HISTORICAL ANECDOTES FROM THE FIRE ISLAND NEWS

by

Thomas McGann

Agapi tis Glossas Publishers logo is a registered trademark of Agapi tis Glossas Publishers

ISBN:

LCCN:

Published by Agapi tis Glossas Publishers, USA

938 Virginia St. #201, Dunedin, FL 34698

For my wife, Donna, who spent thirty years, (year round) on Fire Island, and is well tempered by its pioneer spirit

FOREWORD

It has been my pleasure to work with Thomas McGann at Fire Island News since 2015. Through his wife Donna, I had been acquainted with him more than a decade before that, but I did not know him as "Tom the writer," until he expressed interest in contributing to FIN, which had recently been purchased by new owners. Having taken on professional writing as a second career, he was still new to the craft, but had a lifetime of seasoned experience behind him – an interesting combination.

The question was what would be the best fit for him within our publication? He was not a journalism student, so giving him a reporting beat did not make much sense, and after a few false starts I learned his serious nature meant that he was not cut out for many lifestyle feature assignments either. However he was passionate about writing and my gut told me that giving up on him would be a mistake.

In all fairness, if Tom was trying to find his footing as a writer, so was I as an editor, which was still new to me. We were both in the process of trying to figure out what worked and what did not. That said, some columnists did not come back the following season, and others had to be let go. This was a necessary step but one which, never the less, left us short-handed. By then Tom and Donna had relocated to Florida.

In August of 2016, I called Tom and asked him to do me a favor: The Free Union Church was celebrating its centennial, could he please talk to a few of the church trustees and put together something nice?

What he ended up delivering exceeded all expectations. This was no standard human-interest story about a local church – he had elevated it to something much more substantial. I still remember telephoning him to tell him what an excellent piece it was. He seemed a little surprised.

From then on in, figuring out what articles were going to have his byline became less difficult. Tom needed assignments that were going to be a challenge. In 2017, I asked him to become our history columnist, and he has blossomed there ever since. His talent for research is deft and solid, his sense of humor evident, and he knows how to tell a good story.

Indeed, Tom is sometimes at his very best when he is taken a little bit out of his comfort zone. Difficult topics like the controversial Robert Moses, or Long Island's own Nazi American Bund known as Camp Siegfried were struggles for him, as they would be for any writer, but he dove in unflinchingly, keeping an open mind as to the outcome of his findings.

The hallmark of a fine writer is that they never stop learning, growing or being curious. Thomas McGann has proven time and time again that he is all of those things.

Shoshanna McCollum
Editor, Fire Island News

ACKNOWLEDGEMENTS

I want to acknowledge Shoshanna McCullum, my editor at the Fire Island News, for her inspiring ideas, for her careful critiques, but most of all for her unending support and encouragement. Thank you, Shoshanna.

In addition I would like to thank the following individuals for providing photographs and permission for their use: Susan Barbash, George Bockhart, Jim Betz, Terry Blitman at L.I. Maritime Museum, Tasha Caswell at the Connecticut Historical Society, Melissa Davis at George C. Marshall Foundation, Kurt Dion, Ernie Fazio at Lambda.net, Troy Files at Cherry Grove Archives Collection, John J. Gallagher, at the Longwood Central School District, Dept of Music and Fine Art, Chris Jimenez at Fire Island Wind LLC, Ciri.com, David Joel at Larry Rivers Foundation, and Irving Like's children Bob Like, Sharon Like, and Steven Like, as well as Frank Mina, Matt Pearo of the Manorville Historical SocietyRobert Sherman, of the Utica Observer-Dispatch, Ken Spooner, the William Floyd Estate, Loring Vogel and Bill Weiland. Thank you all

Table of Contents

Source: National Park Service

Fire Is. Inlet

Robert Moses
State Park

LONG ISLAND

Fire Island

Causeway

Fire Island National Seashore
Administrative Boundary

Lighthouse

KISMET
SEABAY BEACH
SALTAIRE
FAIR HARBOR
DUNEWOOD
LONELY WALK
ATLANTIQUE
ROBBINS REST
CORNEILLE ESTATES
OCEAN BEACH
SEAVIEW
OCEAN BAY PARK
POINT O'WOODS
CHERRY GROVE
FIRE ISLAND PINES
WATER ISLAND
DAVIS PARK

Sailors Haven

Talisman

Watch Hill

GREAT SOUTH BAY

Patchogue

MONTAUK HIGHWAY

ATLANTIC OCEAN

FI National Seashore
Wilderness Area
Town
State or County Park

Smith Point
County Park

Moriches Inlet

27A

Rutgers Cartography 2008

0 1 km
0 1 mi

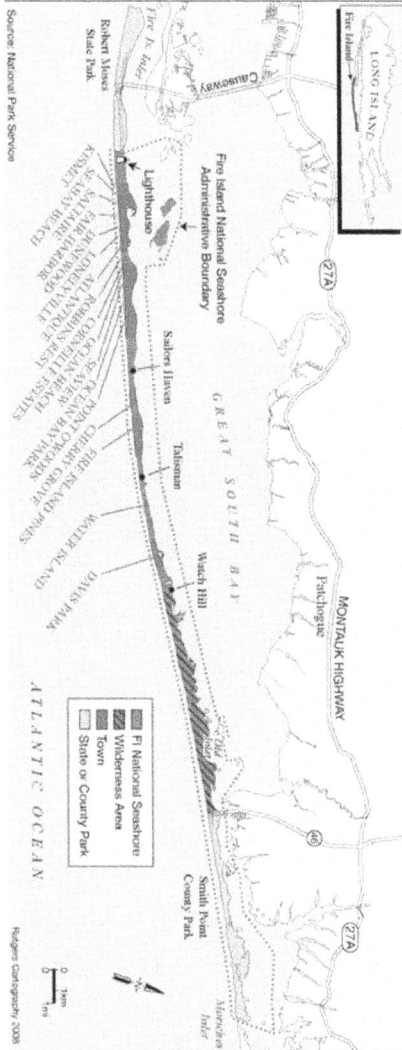

MAP OF FIRE ISLAND

INTRODUCTION

Fire Island is unique—a barrier beach island only sixty miles east of Manhattan, NYC, with the Atlantic Ocean on one side and the Great South Bay on the other providing beautiful beaches in relatively sequestered environments. Even today Fire Island is often referred to as "New York's best kept secret."

There are a number of barrier islands in the U.S. along the East and Gulf Coasts, from Maine to Florida and onto Texas. They are long, narrow spits of sand separating oceans and/or gulfs from the lagoons on their opposite sides.

There has been an ongoing debate for the last 150 years as to how barrier islands are formed with little agreement among scientists as to any definitive answer. What is known is that beach sand moves along the ocean east to west where it builds up on the east side of each inlet. The inlet stays open by moving to the west. The present Fire Island lighthouse, once adjacent to the inlet, now sits about six miles to its east due to sand migration.

Regardless of how they were formed barrier islands provide important functions other than just being sandy beaches on which to cavort in the sun. They absorb energy from ocean waves protecting the coastlines of the mainland, and often provide areas where wetlands can flourish.

Fire Island is part of what is known as the Outer Barrier, aka the Long Island and New York City barrier islands. They consist of Long Beach, Barnum Island, Jones

Beach, Fire Island, and Westhampton Island. This Outer Barrier extends 75 miles, west to east, from Rockaway to Shinnecock. Six inlets separate each of the islands and provide flushing for the lagoons/bays.

FIRE ISLAND

Fire Island is 32 miles long by only one half a mile at its widest and lays about 5 miles off the south shore of Long Island, parallel to it, but it is much more than just a spit of sand. Fourteen major vegetation types or subspecies have been identified on Fire Island including beach grass, heather, bearberry, scrub oaks, pitch-pine woodlands, thickets, broadleaf forest and a variety of wetland and salt marsh plants.

Numerous species of fish are in abundance, stripers, blues, flounder, etc. in addition to oysters, mussels, and clams. Clams and oysters shells are the sources of the white, and most desirable, beads in wampum. Marine mammals include whales, dolphins, harbor seals and porpoises.

There are 17 species of terrestrial mammals that have been identified on Fire Island.: cottontail rabbits, red fox, raccoons, muskrats, numerous species of mice, squirrels, and white tail deer whose numbers continue to grow because of the abundant food supply and lack of native predators.

The deer have become so numerous that they have become a problem. Deer are herbivores and eat a wide variety of vegetation, negatively impacting the island's forests, especially the endangered Holly stand in Sunken Forest. Without predators and with the abundance of food, deer populations can double every two to three years.

DEER ON FIRE ISLAND – LIGHTHOUSE IN
BACKGROUND

Attempts to control the deer population by birth control and managed culling (hunting) are not popular among residents who enjoy the presence of the deer, even hand feeding them which is against the law. It is a growing problem yet to be solved.

The native Americans who lived on Long Island, Paumanok (Isle of Tribute) as they called it, often made trips to Fire Island, Sewanhacky (Isle of Shells) where they hunted whales and seals and engaged in fishing. They visited but created no permanent settlement of which there is any record.

There are presently sixteen established communities on the island but no roads. The island is accessible only by bridges on either extremity that terminate in dead-end state parking lots. The only other access is by commercial ferry systems or private boats.

Prior to 1900 there were probably no permanent residents living on Fire Island with of the exception of the Surfmen of the U.S. Life Saving Service, the lighthouse keeper and his family, and a few scattered squatters. According to the 2010 census there are only about 300 year round residents on the whole island, but the population swells to in excess of 25,000 during the fourteen summer weeks of peak activity. For those permanent residents spread along the length of the island the winters are tests of their pioneer spirit. They can go weeks without seeing another soul, noting their presence only by sightings of footprints in the snow.

This work is a collection of 35 short anecdotes on the history of Fire Island, N.Y. originally published in the Fire Island News between 2015 and 2020 It is followed by three articles that were never published but which I consider important enough to be included here.

These pieces are presented in roughly chronological order allowing for time overlaps. They are not in the order in which they were originally published which oftentimes corresponded to anniversaries of the events covered. A few have been grouped together because of the similarity of content.

I have added back some copy included in the original pieces that had to be cut due to newspaper space constraints. I have also added some additional copy and new photos, and made corrections where new facts were discovered. The font has been changed and typos corrected.

In cases where the article referred to an up and coming event that has since passed, I changed the tense from future to past tense.

Each story is singular, but each builds on the others to illustrate the uniqueness that is Fire Island.

There is an old superstition that once you have slept with F.I. sand in your bed you will always return. Take these stories as grains of sand that sleep in the bed of your mind, begetting dreams and adventures to hasten your arrival, and then sweet reminiscences to encourage many happy returns.

WOMEN'S RIGHTS, AN ITALIAN REVOLUTIONARY AND A SHIPWRECK

Because of its location jutting out into the Atlantic Ocean on the approach to New York harbor, Fire Island is renowned for numerous shipwrecks. On July 19, 1850, a sailing vessel named *Elizabeth* ran aground on a bar near Point O' Woods, five miles east of the present day Fire Island Lighthouse. Eight persons died in that tragedy including the renowned author and feminist Margaret Fuller, her Italian revolutionary husband and their child. This event was the catalyst for the construction of the present day Fire Island Lighthouse, the presence of which has prevented many subsequent tragedies.

Women's Rights

Margaret Fuller was an early women's rights advocate, a believer in prison reform and the emancipation of slaves. She embraced the Transcendentalist movement that was popular in the early 1800s, believing in the goodness of man and nature, and that society and its institutions, such as religion and politics, corrupted man's soul.

She was the author of *Women in the Nineteen Century*, the first major American feminist tract. Other feminists of her generation such as Susan B. Anthony and Elizabeth Cady Stanton credit Fuller, writing that she "was the precursor of the Women's Rights Agitation."

A LARGE EDITION OF THIS ENGRAVED PORTRAIT OF
MARGARET FULLER WAS PRODUCED IN 1850, SHORTLY
AFTER HER PASSING.

She also worked for Horace Greeley at the *New York Tribune* as its first full time book critic of either sex, and then as its first female editor. In 1846, Greeley sent Fuller to Europe, his first female foreign correspondent.

An Italian Revolutionary

In England Fuller met Giuseppe Mazzini, an Italian revolutionary responsible, with Giuseppe Garibaldi, for unifying Italy. Fuller also met Giovanni Ossoli, one of Mazzini's lieutenants, a man ten years her junior, with whom she conducted a passionate love affair resulting in the birth of their child, Angelino.

In 1848, Ossoli fought with Mazzini to establish a Roman Republic, a unified Italy. This particular Italian revolution was short lived however. The Austrians quickly dispatched Mazzini and his cohorts, forcing them into exile.

Ossoli was penniless and on the run with his wife and child. They decided to transit to America where Fuller intended to publish her history of the Italian Revolution. They booked passage on the *Elizabeth*, a 530-ton barque, carrying a cargo of mostly Carrera marble. Prior to embarking, Fuller wrote to a friend "various omens have combined to give me a dark feeling...that my future on earth will soon close...I have a vague expectation of some crisis—I know not what."

SHIPWRECK OF THE *ELIZABETH*

On May 17, 1850, the *Elizabeth* left Livorno, Italy enroute New York carrying five passengers and a crew of 14 under Captain Seth Hasty. The ship was barely a week at sea when the captain came down with smallpox and died soon thereafter. The first mate, one Mr. Bangs, a man of limited experience, assumed command.

After transiting the Atlantic, on July 18 the *Elizabeth* lay just off New York ready to make port the following day when a fierce gale blew down on her. Faulty navigation by the inexperienced captain had placed the *Elizabeth* too close to shore, and at about 3:30 am on July 19 the ship struck a bar broadside. The cargo smashed through the hull flooding the hold. The ship foundered some 200 yards offshore as rain and gale-driven waves swept her decks.

On shore, the U.S. Life Saving Service arrived equipped with a lifeboat and a line-throwing mortar (Lyle gun). They were unable to launch the lifeboat due to the heavy seas. The gale winds, blowing shoreward, prevented all lines fired by their Lyle gun from reaching the deck of the stricken ship.

Sometime later, a large wave lifted the ship, smashing her in two on the bar. Somehow, all the crew and passengers survived, gathering on the forecastle, the only part of the ship still above water. With rescue from shore now impossible, those on shore watched those on the ship with quiet desperation. The ship was so close to shore that, with but a score or so of oar strokes, a lifeboat could have saved them all, but no lifeboat could be launched.

Captain Bangs gave the order for all hands to save themselves. Several of the crew then jumped into the sea, leaving the rest to fend for themselves.

Giovanni Ossoli did not know how to swim, so the three family members clung to each other, trapped, resigned to their deaths. In one final desperate attempt to save the child, the ship's steward snatched the baby from Margaret's arms and leapt into the sea.

Another wave crashed down onto the hull cracking the ship's mast in two, throwing everyone on board into the sea.

THE AFTERMATH

Eight persons perished. The ship's steward and the baby both drowned and their bodies were later recovered. The bodies of Margaret Fuller and Giovanni Ossoli, however, were never found.

Henry David Thoreau, the writer and naturalist famous for his book *Walden*, and his friend Ralph Waldo Emerson, the famous essayist and poet, were both fellow transcendentalists and good friends of Fuller's. Thoreau went to Fire Island at Emerson's urging, to see if he could find the bodies of Fuller and her husband. According to Joan von Mehren in her book *Minerva and the Muse*, Thoreau cut a sad, solitary figure as he walked up and down the barrier beach searching for their bodies. He was unsuccessful. Fuller's manuscript was lost as well.

Emerson subsequently published a best-selling memoir of Fuller that focused on her individuality and her personal life—including her affairs—instead of on her work, for which he was widely criticized.

In 1901, Julia Ward Howe had a memorial to Fuller placed on the beach near where the wreck had occurred. It was washed away by the sea some ten years later.

A RARE VINTAGE POSTCARD IMAGE OF THE MEMORIAL THAT WAS BUILT IN FULLER'S HONOR BEFORE IT WAS WASHED OUT TO SEA.

The uproar caused by the wreck of the *Elizabeth*, and the death of Margaret Fuller and her family, spurred on by her high-powered friends, resulted in Congress allocating monies for a new, higher lighthouse.

This present-day lighthouse stands 168 feet tall, powered by two 1000-watt bulbs, flashing every 7.5 seconds. It has a visibility of 21-24 miles. Between the years 1640 to 1825 there were more than 400 ships reported in distress off Fire Island, but since the completion of the new lighthouse this number of has been drastically reduced —thanks to a women's rights advocate, an Italian revolutionary and the unfortunate shipwreck of the barque *Elizabeth*.

THE FASCINATING HISTORY OF LIGHTHOUSES FROM PHAROS TO FIRE ISLAND

PHAROS LIGHTHOUSE.
One of the wonders of the ancient world.
Painting by Fischer Von Erlach 1721

Each August 7th celebrates National Lighthouse Day. It was on August 7, 1789 that the Bureau of Lighthouses was founded. When President Ronald Reagan signed the bill nearly two hundred years later, he did so in recognition of the incalculable lives and resources saved by the active presence of lighthouses.

Lighthouses have been part of human history from the Pharos Lighthouse in Alexandria, Egypt, to our own Fire Island Lighthouse. These first lights were used as navigational aids and were initially nothing more than bonfires set on the beach to warn sailors of dangerous shoals or to mark channels of safe passage.

Not surprisingly, the first lighthouses provided their light using wood fires atop the structures. Over time wood graduated to coal, then to whale oil and eventually electricity.

The most remarkable of these edifices was the Pharos Lighthouse, one of the Seven Wonders of the Ancient World. It was built in 285 BC on an island at the entrance to the harbor at Alexandria, Egypt. Rising to over 440 ft. tall, it was for centuries one of the tallest man-made structures. It stood for 1,500 years until it was toppled by an earthquake.

The oldest existing lighthouse still in operation is the Tower of Hercules, 180 foot high, built circa A.D.100 by the Roman Emperor Trajan. It is modeled after the Pharos Light and overlooks the NW Spanish coast known as the "Coasta da Morta," the Coast of Death.

The first lighthouse in America was the Boston Light built in 1716. It is the only U.S. lighthouse with an official keeper, Ms. Sally Bowman.

The first lighthouse built on the west coast was the light on Alcatraz Island, home of the infamous prison. The first one illuminated by electricity? Surprise! The Statue of Liberty.

America's first official lighthouse was the Boston Light built on Little Brewster Island in Boston Harbor in 1716, paid for by taxing all international vessels transiting the harbor. Today it is a designated National Historic Landmark and, reputably, haunted by the ghost of an old sailor with a heavy dislike for rock and roll music.

The Boston Light may claim to be the first, but the Sandy Hook Lighthouse in New Jersey is the oldest working lighthouse in the United States.

Although the Boston Light had been built nearly fifty years before Sandy Hook, it was blown up by the British as they retreated after losing the Revolutionary War. It was reconstructed in 1783 leaving Sandy Hook as the oldest originally constructed light. Both are still in operation. The Boston Light remains the last manned lighthouse in America and starting in 2003 boasts the first civilian, and first woman keeper, in Boston Light's history.

How about the Fire Island lighthouse? One theory (among many) of how Fire Island got its name is that fires were often seen on the island—whether it was Native American fires lit to render whale blubber, fires for navigational purposes or "wreckers" ruses.

Wreckers ruses, false fires, were used by land pirates, "wreckers," intent on purposely luring ships aground in order to murder the crews and plunder the ships' holds. The most infamous of these wreckers was a man named Jeremiah Smith, said to be Fire Island's first permanent resident. In the late Eighteenth century he built a driftwood shack somewhere between Cherry Grove and Point O' Woods from which he carried out his dastardly deeds. After a successful looting he would transport his pillage, hidden under several layers of quahogs, (clams) to the mainland in his boat for sale to all too willing buyers.

While the Montauk Point Lighthouse was the first Long Island lighthouse and the first federally funded, the Fire Island Light, constructed in 1826, was the second. It was 74 feet tall with the focal plane of its lantern only 89 feet above sea level so its light could be seen no more than 10-14 nautical miles out to sea. As limited as its visibility was it was still the single most important light for transatlantic shipping as it was the first light seen when arriving and the last when departing. The station cost $9,999.65 to build (about $225,000 in today's money) and came in thirty-five cents under budget.

In July of 1850, the barque *Elizabeth* ran aground off Point O' Woods. On board was the feminist writer Margaret Fuller. She, her Italian revolutionary husband, their baby, and five others perished. The resulting uproar, spurred on by Fuller's high-powered friends (Horace Greeley, Henry Thoreau, Ralph Waldo Emerson), resulted in Congress allocating enough funds for building a taller, more effective lighthouse.

"FIRE ISLAND LIGHTHOUSE"
By vishwaant - CC BY 2.0 Copy

Our present lighthouse was built following John Smeaton's prototypic Eddystone Rocks design (it is said that an oak tree was his inspiration), a circular structure, wide at its base, tapering toward its top. The interior is a constant 10.5 feet, but the walls vary in thickness from 11 feet at the base to 2.5 feet at its top. It was built of red brick, painted a creamy-yellow color and was completed in 1858. The tower was repainted with its present-day black and white bands in 1891.

With a focal plane of 168 feet above sea level its visibility is now 21-24 nautical miles. It was originally equipped with a state of the art, first order (largest available) Fresnel lens using a whale oil lamp that rotated emitting a 5 second flash once every minute.

Back then there were no roads or bridges to Fire Island, (the Robert Moses Causeway was not completed until 1964) so perhaps it was the isolation of the island that generated some odd behavior on the part of its Lightkeepers. One Felix Dominy openly welcomed visitors, providing accommodations at the lighthouse, affording him and his wife company, relieving their boredom. Regulations allowed Lightkeepers to serve "spuretts and things accordeen," so the Dominy's became innkeepers of sorts serving liquor and victuals to their guests. They later built an inn that lasted until Felix Dominy died at which time Pheobe. Dominy open a hotel in Bay Shore.

Keeper Hans Andersen was so lonely he advertised for a wife, describing himself as "a stoutly built man of 38 with a jolly face and mustache." Andersen selected a wife from the 250 or so respondents and fathered two children with her. Love conquers all.

Another keeper, Seth Hubbard, became a wrecker. He was caught with property stolen from the passenger liner *Oregon*—289 yards of fine lace, twelve black silk shawls, fifty-six neckties, fifty-two handkerchiefs and a quantity of silverware, enough to "stock a Broadway store." He was also accused of receiving kickbacks on services and provisions. Evidently he was so busy with his side ventures that he allowed the light to go out. He and his son-in-law were fired.

In the 18th century kerosene replaced whale oil as the primary fuel. Early in the twentieth century the original Fresnel lens was replaced with one much lighter and the light frequency was increased to a flash every 7.5 seconds instead of every minute. It was later replaced with a Crouse-Hinds beacon. Electricity arrived when the Coast Guard assumed responsibility for the Light and a cable was laid across the Great South Bay.

Because of its deteriorating condition, the Fire Island Lighthouse was decommissioned on New Year's Eve 1973. In its place a flashing strobe light was affixed to the top of the Robert Moses State Park's landmark water tower.

By 1981 the lighthouse was declared unsafe and was scheduled to be torn down, but the Fire Island Lighthouse Preservation Society (FILPS) was formed to preserve and restore the lighthouse. By 1989 FILPS had raised over a million dollars, renovated the light and opened it to the public, fittingly, on August 7th—National Lighthouse Service Bicentennial celebration day.

FILPS also built a museum to house the original 9,000 lb, sixteen-foot tall Fresnel lens in a structure that replicates its old steam power generating building. A United States Lifesaving Service exhibit is in a nearby boathouse. The Crouse-Hinds beacon can be seen at the lighthouse visitor's center museum, the original Lightkeepers quarters.

Come visit. Climb to the top of the lighthouse to see how far you can see. There are 192 steps, (including nine up a ladder to the Light Room). Given the curvature of the Earth and the refraction of our atmosphere, you should be able to see maybe 20 or so miles.

Given the curve of history, if you concentrate hard enough, you may be able to spot the fires of Native Americans rendering whale blubber or the fires of those vile wreckers—either of which (or both) may have given the island its name.

More than 100,000 guests visit the lighthouse and its complements each year. The fees provide for its maintenance and operational expenses. Adult tickets cost $10 (2021), seniors and children twelve years and under are $5. Please allow at least 2 hours for your visit, it's that interesting. Call 631-661-4876 for more information.

FRESNEL LENS – THE INVENTION THAT SAVED A MILLION SHIPS

Long Island is home to some 20 odd lighthouses. Montauk Point Light was the first built, but Fire Island Light is the tallest at 168 feet (with 182 steps—but who's counting) and is 50 feet higher than her sister out at Montauk. In addition to the Fire Island lighthouse itself with its stunning 360-degree views from the gallery platform at its top, the compound also boasts a museum and gift shop in the converted Lighthouse Keepers quarters. Not to be overlooked is the Fresnel lens housed in a spectacular building built specifically for its display.

HISTORICAL ACTOR JOSEPH SMITH IN CHARACTER
AS AUGUSTIN-JEAN FRESNEL AT A PERFORMANCE AT THE
FIRE ISLAND LIGHTHOUSE LEND BUILDING IN 2017
. (PHOTO BY SHOSHANNA MCCOLLUM)

The Fresnel lens was the "soul of the lighthouse," a 16-foot high, pineapple-shaped lens that focused the light rays from the lantern room atop the tower, through heavy glass panels called storm panes, out to sea.

Often called "the invention that saved a million ships," this marvel of a lens is an invention of the French physicist Augustin-Jean Fresnel (1788-1827).

Fresnel was fascinated by light and spent his short life developing theories on its propagation. His research in optics, specifically the wave theory of light, overshadowed even Isaac Newton. But it is the Fresnel lens for which he is mostly remembered.

There was a need for some sort of lens to concentrate the rays of light into a single beam that could be seen at great distances by ships navigating off shore waters. In 1819, the French Commission of Lighthouses asked scientists for possible improvements in lighthouse illumination. Several scientists tinkered with the idea, but it was Fresnel's design of a thin, lightweight lens in the form of a multi-part unit mounted in a frame that changed history.

His idea was an array of prisms, arranged in a circle, each ground to a different angle. This collected disparate rays and focused them into a single beam. Additionally, his design of multiple lenses with large apertures and short focal lengths enabled its construction using much less material than previous designs.

His first prototype, which he called "lenses by steps," so impressed the commission that he was assigned to produce a full-scale version. A year later, in 1821, an official test of his newest light was witnessed by Louis

XVIII and his entourage from 32 kilometers away, and was so impressive that the following summer the world's first lighthouse equipped with a Fresnel lens was lit.

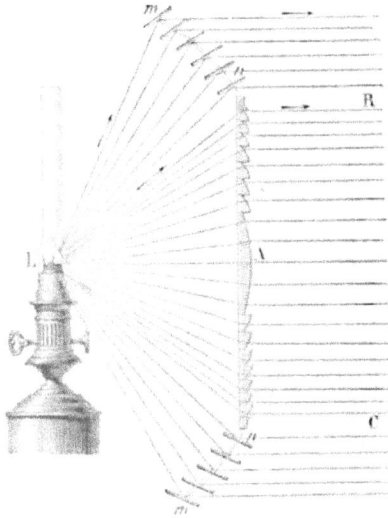

THE FRESNEL LENS

Fresnel continued his lighthouse work despite the fragility of his health (he had started coughing up blood). He resigned from numerous projects on which he had been working to concentrate on lenses for lighthouses which, at this point, he considered his most important work. Fresnel designed six sizes of lenses divided into four orders determined by size and focal length. The largest were called first-order lenses. He also laid out a map for 51 lighthouses, and lesser lights, using lenses of varying sizes

23

depending on their application. Augustin-Jean Fresnel died on Bastille Day in 1827 of tuberculosis at age 39.

Fresnel remains one of the geniuses associated with the likes of Isaac Newton, Christiaan Huygnes, and Blaise Pascal. His name is one of 72 engraved on the base of the Eiffel Tower. Several features on the moon have also been named after him. One of his contemporaries, Humphrey Lloyd, provost of Trinity College, Dublin, described his work as "the noblest fabric which has ever adorned the domain of physical science, Newton's system of the universe alone excepted." Fresnel was granted the Royal Society's Rumford Medal on his deathbed.

The current Fire Island Lighthouse was outfitted with a state-of-the-art revolving first-order Fresnel lens upon its completion in 1858, and it remained in operation until the U.S Coast Guard removed it in 1933and it was placed on extended loan to Philadelphia's Franklin Institute.

For 75 years it was the first light sighted by millions of immigrants reaching America's shores.

Aug. 7 is National Lighthouse Day, an opportune occasion to come see Fire Island's own famous lighthouse. After a long closure due to the corona virus it is again open to the public. Don't forget to visit the Fresnel lens during your visit to celebrate its rightful return back home on Fire Island Lighthouse grounds.

THE WILLIAM FLOYD ESTATE – GUNPOWDER AND GUMPTION

The William Floyd Estate is one of the gems of the Fire Island National Seashore. The Estate is the ancestral home of William Floyd (1734-1821), one of only 56 original signers of the Declaration of Independence.

WILLIAM FLOYD
The Metropolitan Museum of Art/Public Domain

The Estate is not contiguous with the rest of the FI National Seashore. It sits on 613 acres of forest, fields and marsh land approximately 2 mile south of Sunrise Hwy in Mastic Beach, LI fronting both Narrow and Moriches Bays. It contains the "Old Mastic House", and twelve out buildings reflecting three centuries of early American life.

The estate has an interesting, if somewhat convoluted, history.

The English born William "Tangier" Smith (1655-1705) had been mayor of Tangier, Morocco (hence his nickname) and was granted patents (land grants) in America in recognition of his service to the Crown. He added extensive purchases of various Indian lands until by 1697 he had accumulated more than 81,000 acres, stretching from the Southampton Town line to Shirley; from Rte 25 in the north to the Atlantic Ocean in the south, including 24 miles of Great South Barrier Beach now known as Fire Island.

In about 1656 Richard Floyd, William Floyd's great-grandfather, emigrated from Wales to America. In 1718 his son and namesake purchased 4,400 acres from the Tangier Smith family. That acreage included all the "beach, meadow, and bay" stretching six mile north from Moriches Bay to one mile west of the Forge River and included Fire Island.

Both families, Smiths and Floyds, built homes a mere three miles apart, the Manor of St. George, and the Old Mastic House.

With the death of Wm. Tangier Smith his property was divided between his sons. His Setauket estate, being considered the more valuable, was inherited by his oldest son while the Mastic property was left to the second oldest.

Meanwhile, Nichol Floyd inherited his property from his father Richard and proceeded to build the first portion of the Old Mastic House, a six room, two-story, wood frame home. It was completed about 1724. Nichol Floyd cleared and planted the lands and made it into a prosperous plantation, expanding the home as his wealth and the family grew. He and his wife had nine children and in 1755 both died of typhoid fever.

Upon his death he left the property to his oldest son, William Floyd, signer of the Declaration of Independence.

WILLIAM FLOYD HOUSE
Lfstar68- Creative Commons Attribution-Share Alike 3.0 Unported

Floyd married twice. He had 3 children by his first wife Hannah Jones who died in 1781 and 2 children with his second wife, Joanna Strong.

Mary Floyd, William Floyd's eldest daughter, married Col. Benjamin Tallmadge in the Old Mastic House. Tallmadge will later play a major role in the fate of the Manor of St. George.

William Floyd became active in politics becoming a delegate in both the First and Second Continental Congresses. In the Old Mastic House he hosted the likes of

Thomas Jefferson, James Madison and the Marquis de Lafayette.

But Americans were chaffing under the yoke of British policies particularly taxation without representation. Sparked by the Stamp Act in 1765, followed by the Boston Massacre, and the battle of Lexington and Concord, the Founding Fathers first drafted and then signed the Declaration of Independence on July 4th, 1776 (most scholars assign August 2nd as the actual date). William Floyd was the first of the New York delegates to sign.

These days we celebrate the signing of the Declaration of Independence by going to the beach, playing ballgames, and burning backyard BBQs with scarcely a thought of how momentous that act really was. Only 56 men signed the document and by doing so they were guilty of treason, putting their lives on the line. That's a lot of gumption, guts and grit.

About the singing, Benjamin Franklin later is quoted as having said, "We must, indeed, all hang together or, most assuredly we shall all hang separately."

But the last sentence of the Declaration of Independence says it best. "And for the support of this Declaration, with a firm reliance on the protection of Divine Providence, we mutually pledge to each other our Lives, our Fortunes, and our sacred Honor."

Dwell on *sacred honor* for a moment – or two.

During the Revolutionary War both the Old Mastic House and the Manor of St. George were occupied by British military forces. William Floyd's estate was occupied by a company of horsemen for the remainder of the war, and Floyd and his family were forced to flee to

Connecticut. Judge Wm. Smith III (of the Smith line) took his family to Kingston, NY after the British had garrisoned the Manor of St. George.

The Manor was also the site of a glorious American victory. Recognizing its strategic location, a few hundred yards from ocean access at Smith Inlet, a deep-water channel nearly a half-mile wide at the time, the British built a triangular fort surrounding the Manor using stockade fencing 12 ft. high.

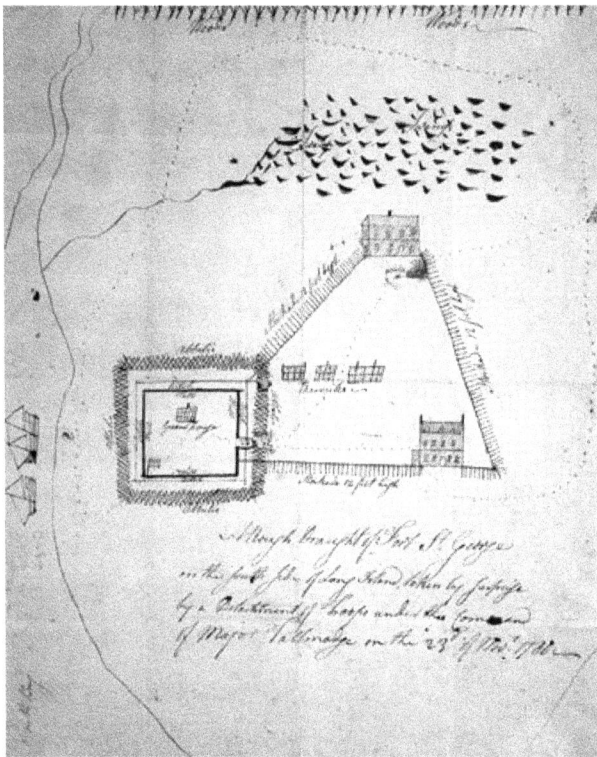

SKETCH OF MANOR ST. GEORGE, DONE FOR THE
BATTLE OF FORT ST. GEORGE.
Courtesy of Connecticut Historical Society

Benjamin Tallmadge, the man who married Wm. Floyd's daughter, was one of the leaders of George Washington's Culper spy ring (as reported here in the Fire Island News—you dare not miss an issue!) He raised a force of 80 unhorsed dragoons who rowed whaleboats for five hours, 15 miles across the LI Sound. They then marched 20 miles across LI in a drenching rainstorm that forced them to delay their attack until their gunpowder dried. At first light they hacked their way through the stockade fence shouting "Washington and glory!" and, after a brief firefight, captured the fort.

BENJAMIN TALLMADGE
Public Domain

Using British cannons and gunpowder, Tallmadge turned the guns on a British warship lying at anchor in the bay and sank it. He then burned down both the fort and the Manor of St. George, a haven for British officers.

He then chose a party of 12, commandeered British horses, and rode to Coram where they set fire to a strategic store of hay the British had provisioned there. The next morning they rowed home without the loss of a single American life, with ample stolen supplies and several prisoners.

After peace was restored by the 1783 Treaty of Paris, William Floyd returned to Mastic to find his plantation nearly destroyed, stripped of all its crops, livestock, timber and household goods. He restored the plantation while about the same time the Smiths rebuilt the Manor of St. George.

Supposedly there have been three generations of St. George manor houses—the original house, the house destroyed during the Revolutionary War, and the existing home said to have been built about 100-125 feet from the present house. The Manor House and the William Floyd House exist today about 2½ to 3 miles apart in Mastic.

William Floyd was involved in politics for much of his life. He often served as presidential elector, was a member of the New York State Senate, and was elected to Congress in the first election under our new Constitution. Upon retirement he held the rank of Major General in the NYS Militia but toward the end of his life he devoted his time to his new farm along the Mohawk River in Westernville, upstate NY. He passed away in 1821 at the age of 86 and is buried there, although his original headstone remains in Mastic.

The Old Mastic House was passed down through nine generations. William Floyd's great-great-granddaughter, Cornelia Floyd, donated it to the National Park Service in 1976 and it has been meticulously maintained with few changes ever since.

The Old Mastic House showcases the building's unique combination of Colonial, Victorian and Greek Revival architectural styles. Walk through its 25 rooms and celebrate 300 years of American history from its original post and beam construction, to its 18th century doors, and its 12 over 12 windows. The exhibit features beautiful ceramics, glassware, textiles, documents, etc. that span the centuries.

The original deed for the property is on display— without the purchase price which remains unknown to this day. There is much to see and learn by taking the one hour tour, which includes the "Vista View," still providing its spectacular panorama of the Great South Bay and Fire Island. Keep your eyes out for wild Turkeys!

The house is open every Friday-Sunday, and Federal holidays, from Memorial Day weekend through Veterans Day. Tours start at 10 am and run to 4 pm every half-hour. The tours are free.

In 2018 the first ever historic marker was dedicated to the Old Mastic House. The marker is a gift from the Narrow Bay Historical Society. Musicians strolled about the grounds playing a variety of colonial and/or civil war songs.

An anniversary cake-cutting followed at noon with light refreshments. Tours were conducted as normal and.

monumental history was made in the Old Mastic House that day.

It is definitely worth a visit.

THE TWO OTHER HALVES –
BROKEN IN TWO - WILLIAM
FLOYD'S WIVES

It just does not seem fair that all the glory goes to the men while their wives get short shrift.

General William Floyd (1734-1821), one of only 56 signers of the Declaration of Independence, had two homes and was married twice. The first home is the William Floyd Estate in Mastic, NY, part of the Fire Island National Seashore. His first wife was Hannah Jones (1740-1781), daughter of William and Mary (née?) Jones of Southampton.

His second home is the General William Floyd House in Westernville, NY. His second wife was Joanna Strong, (1747-1826), daughter of Benajah and Martha (Mills) Strong, of Setauket, NY.

He also has two gravestones, a large monument in Westernville and a ground slab in Mastic.

What little is known of Floyd's wives can be read in the few brief entries on the internet and in the brief, but interesting, book "A Portrait of William Floyd, Long Islander" by William Quentin Maxwell.

William Floyd married Hannah Jones on August 20, 1760. She was a "public-spirited and patriotic woman" who supported her husband's various pursuits. From the moment Floyd began to take part in public life, Hannah was left with the management of his affairs including running the Mastic plantation.

And she did a damn good job!

By 1767, they had three children. The son, Nicoll Floyd, the oldest of the children, married Phebe Gelston of New York. The oldest daughter, Mary Floyd (affectionately called Polly), married Colonel Benjamin Tallmadge of Litchfield, Connecticut (of Culper Spy Ring/war hero fame, as portrayed in the television mini-series "Turn: Washington's Spies). The younger daughter, Catherine (affectionately called Kitty), married Dr. Samuel Clarkson of Philadelphia.

This is how women are remembered—by whom they married and by their children.

During the Revolutionary War and after the battle of Long Island (which the Americans lost) the British became the occupying force in the area. Long Island was no longer a safe place to be if you were sympathetic to the revolutionary cause, and was an especially dangerous place for a woman whose husband had just signed the Declaration of Independence.

Hannah Floyd barely had time to bury the family silver before she and her three young children, with a few friends and neighbors, sailed across Long Island Sound. They chose Connecticut as their refuge because it was close and it was easier to cross the Long Island Sound than to travel overland.

Hannah took refuge with friends in Middletown, Connecticut and enrolled her son and two daughters in school there. Floyd came to visit whenever he could excuse himself from his duties in Congress.

Hannah would never live to see her Long Island home again. Whatever anxieties and hardships she suffered undermined her health. She died May 16, 1781 at the age of 41.

Unfortunately, this is where recorded history abandons poor Hannah. She would die while separated from both her home and her husband and become a relatively obscure casualty of the American Revolution.

Even less is known about Floyd's second wife. In 1783, two years after the death of his first wife, General Floyd married Joanna Strong (1747- 1826), daughter of Benajah and Martha (Mills) Strong of Setauket, L. I., by whom he had two more children. Ann, the oldest, married George W. Clinton, son of the Vice-President serving under Thomas Jefferson's second term. She later married Abraham Varick of New York. Eliza, the youngest, married James Platt of Utica.

General William Floyd died August 24, 1821 at his second home in Westernville, NY and is buried in the cemetery behind the Westernville Presbyterian Church. His original gravestone is rectangular in shape and was made to rest horizontally on four stone supports, giving the marker a tomb-like appearance.

The General's second wife, Johanna, outlived him by some five years, and had a similar marker. Though little is known of Joanna she, but not Hannah, has the honor of being buried next to the General.

TOMBSTONE ENGRAVED WITH WILLIAM FLOYD'S
NAME AS WELL AS BOTH WIVES
Photo courtesy of Kurt Deion / kurtshistoricsites.com

Both of these tombstones remained at Westernville cemetery until 1895 when a larger, more elaborate monument was erected in honor of General Floyd's deserved accomplishments. The General's original stone (the tomb-like slab) was moved three hundred miles south to his previous estate in Mastic where it remains on display today with the disclaimer that he is actually buried upstate in Westernville. Johanna's original stone will be on display at the future General William Floyd Center.

But what happened to Floyd's first wife, Hannah? Where is she buried?

Russ Marriott and his wife Jackie are the caretakers/owners of The General William Floyd House in Westernville, N.Y. As "caretakers" they are very passionate about the restoration and preservation of the house. As they so eloquently state on their website, the "history of the

General and his home are not the property of the owners, but are the property of all of us as Americans."

RUSS AND JACKIE MARRIOTT STAND IN FRONT OF
THEIR WESTERNVILLE HOME, WHICH IS THE HISTRORIC
HOME OF DECLARATION OF INDEPENDENCE SIGNER
GENERAL WILLIAM FLOYD ON FRIDAY, JUNE 17, 2011.
Courtesy of Utica Observer-Dispatch

And they mean exactly what they say.

Through the grapevine they heard about the burial site of Hannah Jones and decided to see if they could find her. The local library gave them the directions to the Mortimer cemetery, and made arrangements for them to get the keys to its gate from the neighboring fire station. Unfortunately, it was mid-February and a freak storm had frozen the gate's lock preventing their entry. The Fire Chief came to their rescue. He sent out one of his recruits to help, and the Marriotts were eventually able to explore the cemetery.

They searched the cemetery in the snow on freezing feet with darkness closing in before, literally, stumbling on Hannah Jones' gravestone. Lying at their feet was a small, weatherworn stone. It had but three words on it, "Mrs. Hannah Floyd." It was broken in two.

It had broken in two and no one noticed, or cared, for all those years. She has been moved to the General's grave site.

Today, there are hundreds of descendents of General Floyd and his two wives. The irony of it all is that the DNA of the wives flows through the same veins of each and every one of these descendants as does that of the General, and will be carried forward onto future generations just like his.

Viva les femmes!

LONG ISLAND RAIL ROAD HISTORY AND FIRE ISLAND

Besides the obvious—beaches, beauty, and solitude—a major reason Fire Island is so popular is its proximity to New York City and its environs, drawing on a population of 12 million people within a 50 mile radius. Its draw is also the ease of access for those who choose Fire Island for their getaway, the ability to get there in reasonable amounts of time with as little hassle as possible. The Long Island Rail Road (LIRR) and the various ferries that leave from the few strategic communities along Long Island's south shore provide this access.

The LIRR local from Penn Station in Manhattan to Bay Shore/Sayville ordinarily takes about 90 minutes. An express train can take as little as 70 minutes. Then a short jaunt by taxi to the ferry terminal, and then a usually beautiful, mind-clearing half-hour boat ride to the island access you to a whole new world.

Access has always been a top priority, even early on in Fire Island history.

Back in 1855 David Sammis purchased 120 acres east of the Fire Island Lighthouse and erected the world famous Surf Hotel. At its peak, the hotel accommodated 1500 guests, the rich and famous, and, of course, many politicians. With its gas lamps and telegraph, it took its place among the top most celebrated resorts on the Atlantic coast.

But Sammis had to get his guests to the island. The Southside railroad, a competitor of the LIRR, had service from NYC to Deer Park by 1867 but Sammis still had to get his guests from the train station to the dock, a four mile trip, by stagecoach. This was followed by a sail out to the island—whatever the weather—no small endeavor even for the hardiest.

Later the Southside Railroad had tracks out to Babylon which then became known as the "Gateway to Fire Island." Extensions to the line reached Sayville in 1868 and Patchogue in 1869.

Undaunted, in 1871 Sammis built his own "Babylon Railroad," a trolley line from the Babylon train station, down Fire Island Avenue, to his now steamboat dock. The trolley, running on rails, was first horse-drawn, then steam powered, and finally electrical when it became available. His personal steam yacht then carried them to Fire Island, a trip that took, in total from NYC, not much more than two hours.

By 1869 the Southside Railroad was taken over by the LIRR and its rails are now the main branch running from either Penn Station and/or Flatbush Ave in Brooklyn all the way out to Montauk..

The history of America's rail road industry follows that of most startup businesses. In 1826, the railways established themselves as the transportation fix for the future, albeit mostly covering only short distances, often using different gauge track. As the industry expanded, inefficient lines were consolidated within larger companies, until 1906 when seven entities, owned by men like J.P. Morgan, Cornelius Vanderbilt, and Jay Gould, controlled two-thirds of the countries railroads. One of these was the Pennsylvania Rail Road (PRR), which became, for a time, the largest corporation in the world with a budget in excess of that of the U.S. government. The corporation paid out dividends for over a hundred years, a record that remains unbroken to this day. In 1906 the PRR absorbed the LIRR.

One of America's first major railways was the Baltimore and Ohio (B&O). It used horses to pull the train cars until the advent of steam in 1829.

The first American locomotive was called the "Tom Thumb," a coal-fired, vertical boiler steam engine whose tubes were rifle barrels. In a race between a horse and the locomotive, the horse won when "Tom Thumb" broke down. Even so, steam was here to stay.

The original, and rather audacious, LIRR plan was for a rail line that would provide daily commuter service from Brooklyn all the way to Boston with a steamship connection from Greenport on Long Island's north fork to Stonington, Ct where passengers would pick up the Boston-Providence Rail Road for the final leg into Boston. The estimated time for this trip was 11 hours—not bad for 1834. Before this endeavor could be completed, however, the New York, New Haven and Hartford rail line was built over "impassable" southern Connecticut to provide service from NY to Providence and eventually Boston, negating the need for the Greenport to Stonington connection..

One of the first lengths of track built on Long Island was for the Brooklyn and Jamaica Rail Road (B&J), a ten mile stretch from the East River to Jamaica. It was immediately subsumed by the LIRR to complement its line originating in Williamsburg, Brooklyn. The main line continued to be Brooklyn to Greenport. Its first run was completed in July 1844, a journey that took only 3½ hours. Today's schedule allots 3hrs and 5min for the same trip.

Meanwhile, additional branches were being built by various entrepreneurs trying to carve out market niches for themselves. One line reached Hicksville in 1837, Hempstead in 1839, Deer Park in 1841 and Millville (Yaphank) in 1844. Nearby residents in Huntington and Babylon had to take stagecoaches to these stations.

One of these competitors was known as the South Side Railway, consolidated in 1860, authorized to run along the south shore of Long Island as far as Islip. In 1867 its charter was extended out to East Hampton. Regular service to Seaside (Babylon) began in October of 1867 and to Patchogue in April of 1869, but often had to rely on other railroads (Brooklyn Central for one) and/or horse cars to complete the trip.

The line pushed its way further east, establishing a Sag Harbor Branch, now called the Montauk Branch. It opened in 1869, running from St. George's Manor (Manorville) to Hampton Bays, extending to Sag Harbor and Bridgehampton in 1870, and finally Montauk in 1895.

The hamlet of Manorville was once part of a land grant given to Col. William "Tangier" Smith in 1693 for his service as governor of Tangiers, Morocco. Called the Manor Saint George, it was an enormous tract of land, reaching from present day Mastic all the way to Southampton, from the Atlantic Ocean in the south, to Rte 25 (Calverton) in the north, including some 50 miles of barrier beach including Fire Island.

The Long Island Rail Road in competition with the South Side Railway ran its tracks into Manorville in 1844, to a station then called Manor St. George. The station agent, a revolutionary war patriot named Seth Raynor was so incensed at the reference to St. George, the patron saint of England and its monarchy, (so the story goes) that when his wife was painting their fence, Seth grabbed a brush and painted over the words "St. George" leaving the name of the station as "Manor." It stuck, becoming Manor Station in 1852, and with the opening of the post office in 1907, officially as Manorville.

FORMER MANORVILLE LIRR STATION
Courtesy of Manorville Historical Society

On November 8, 1867, an article in the Brooklyn Eagle newspaper described the opening of the South Side Railway in part, as follows:

"The South Side Railroad which has been pushed forward with commendable energy is now open for travel from Jamaica to Sayville, a distance of forty-one miles. By this road a productive section of Long Island is brought within easy access of Brooklyn and New York, adding millions to the value of the property on the Island and in this city, if we are not blinder than bats to our own interests ...If we are wise enough to secure a desirable terminus for this road in Brooklyn, thousands of honest toilers, now confined in pent up apartments, may secure homes within reach of their business, and a few acres of honest earth which they can call their own."

The newspaper goes on to describe, if not so rhapsodically, the various stations along its route with such foreign names as Pearsall's Corner (Lynbrook), "within five miles of the popular bathing resort of Far Rockaway," Baldwinville, Seaside (Babylon), and Penaticutt/Penataquit/Mechanicsville (Bayshore.)

The paper continues, in no uncertain terms, that its interest is really in the benefits this new railway system would provide Brooklyn.

"The folly of diverting the trade of Long Island is so apparent that it can hardly be necessary to waste words or space upon it. Those who come after us will find it hard to believe for ever [sic] a generation, after steam has been introduced, we saw the produce of the island carted by our very doors, while we were content to follow it to New York, and purchase it when it had lost its freshness, and after

three or four classes of hucksters had made a profit upon it ... In the kitchen is embraced an important department of domestic economy, and no man who is not a candidate for the lunatic asylum, would provide pictures of his parlor while destitute of the means of properly cooking a beef-steak below stairs." [The place where the servants lived and worked—possibly the basement.]

And the paper was not done. The column goes on to extol the pleasures that await their readers brought on by this new railway.

"The summer travel upon it can hardly fail in being immense for the road will connect with many of the most popular bathing and fishing resorts on the south side of the island. Passengers to Rockaway, by taking the cars to Pearsall's Corner (Lynbrook), will have an easy stage ride of less than five miles."

In 1875-76 a wealthy rubber baron, and owner of the Flushing and North Side Rail Road, named Conrad Poppenhusen acquired all the railroads on Long Island and consolidated them into the network we now recognize as the LIRR, and we now have our own horse-power stagecoaches (taxis) for rides from the LIRR to the ferries servicing Fire Island.

The Long Island Rail Road, chartered in 1834, is the second oldest (after the Strasburg Rail Road in PA) U.S. railroad still operating under its original name. It provides service 24/7, year-round, transporting nearly 350,000 passengers every weekday making it the busiest commuter railroad in North America.

LIRR trains may run late occasionally and may not always be as clean as the public might like, but a well deserved thank you should be nodded in the direction of those who made possible such easy access to this sliver of paradise called Fire Island.

This article was originally published under the title "Long Island Rail Road's History with Fire Island" on pages 44 and 45 in the print edition Fire Island News on July 7, 2017.

THE BIZARRE HISTORY OF THE SMITH POINT BRIDGE

Fire Island is accessible by bridges at either end of the island or by boat. The more well-known of the two bridges is the Fire Island Inlet Bridge, sometimes incorrectly referred to as the Robert Moses Bridge because it is a continuation of the Robert Moses Causeway and ends in Robert Moses State Park.

The lesser known of the two bridges, the one with the bizarre history, is the Smith Point Bridge. It extends William Floyd Parkway south from the Smith Point peninsula onto a quarter mile long span over the Narrows between Bellport Bay to its west and Moriches Bay to its east. It terminates in Smith Point County Park.

The land on which the Smith Point Bridge is built was originally part of the William "Tangier" Smith holdings of 81,000 acres, including 24 miles of Great South Barrier Beach now known as Fire Island. In 1718 Richard Floyd purchased 4,400 acres from the Tangier Smith family. It included Smith Point peninsula and three miles of oceanfront beach. There was no bridge.

And then along came *Quimby*, Fredrick J. *Quimby* to be exact or...hmmm...or was it spelled *Quinby*? Official documents differ as to the spelling of the man's name (was it with an "m" or an "n"?) no one was ever quite sure—but there were no doubts as to his grandiose plans.

In either 1910 or 11 Quimby/Quinby (let's just call him "Q") purchased anywhere from 4000 to 10,000 acres (depending on which press release you believe) from the descendants of the Smith family. He touted his plans for turning the property he now called Tangier Manor into "The World's Greatest Development," aka "The Greatest Development of the Century" and offered plots of land for sale.

As incentives to buyers, "Q" promised to dredge a canal across Rockaway Neck (Far Rockaway) to provide a deepwater channel for passage of the yachts of the rich and famous who were invited to stay at his oceanfront Grand Hotel affixed "with structural features unique to itself." It was to compete with the Surf Hotel on western Fire Island and with a distant Atlantic City, N.J. with its boardwalks and oceanfront hi-rise hotels. But "Q" needed a bridge to get to the beach to complete the dream.

AN ARTIST'S RENDITION OF THE PROPOSED
TANGIER BRIDGE AS SEEN BY THE EXTRAVAGANT
IMAGINATION OF FREDRICK QUIMBY.
Photo courtesy of Spoonercentral.com

The construction of a "great drawbridge to span the Great South Bay to join the mainland of Tangier to the beach" was his answer. It would be "a lift structure 350 feet long, 72 feet wide and 75 feet above high water. The arches would be high enough to permit the passing of all but the largest vessels. The invisible lift would make the passage of big steamers and sailing vessels possible."

"Q" hired Michael Gillespie, a recent Irish immigrant, to clear a 215 foot wide "main boulevard" using horse plows. It was to extend four miles from the "Tangier" railway station (LIRR, Montauk line) to the tip of the Tangier peninsula where the bridge was to be built. That road is now the present day William Floyd Parkway.

In all, "Q" invested $4.5 million dollars in his ventures, but he needed an infusion of new cash to keep his head above water. So, on Sunday May 7, 1911 "Q" hired a "Special Train" to transport high rollers from Penn Station to the Tangier station, located between Brookhaven and Mastic. Cars picked up the guests from the train station and drove them to the "Inn-in-the-Pines" where a sumptuous dinner was served. After dinner automobiles transported the guests south to the Narrows where they embarked on motor yachts to sail them across the bay to "Tangier beach, a long stretch of magnificent oceanfront."

Evidently there were not enough takers, and "Q's" endeavor fell into financial distress. Numerous lawsuits had been filed, some going back as early as 1904. One lawsuit was filed by none other than Michael Gillespie. "Q" had stiffed him out of $426 dollars for his work creating the new road to the beach. Newspaper articles about the Tangier property all but disappeared from print, and those that were published mentioned that not much property development was underway.

"Q" tried a $2 million dollar refinance scheme in 1912, but filed for bankruptcy in 1913.

He fled to Virginia and was unable to appear in court, his lawyer said, because he was "very ill." The attorneys on both sides of the lawsuit called each other liars and almost came to blows inside the courthouse. His ex-wife was arrested for threatening to get a gun and shoot him. In 1914 he pawned his wife's jewelry. She later caught him in bed with another woman. Luckily, this was not the same wife with the gun.

THE ACTUAL TANGIER BRIDGE AS BUILT BY MICHAEL GILLESPIE. NOTE THE BASCULE DRAW BRIDGE MECHANISM JUST TO THE LEFT OF QUIMBY'S "GRAND HOTEL"
Photo courtesy of Brookhaven Town Historian.

Somehow or other "Q" raised enough money by 1916 to pay off Gillespie and get him to build a "temporary" Tangier Bridge over to the beach. But it wound up only as a wooden footbridge and put the lie to the opulence described by "Q" in his advertisements. It did have an engine driven drawbridge, the "first access," he bragged, by which the beach could be reached other than by boat.

The bridge did not last long however. Early in 1917, two hundred feet in the center of the bridge, including the bascule draw and all its machinery, was destroyed by an ice jam. Subsequent winter storms continued to ravage the remains of the bridge.

In 1924, a Patchogue fisherman tied his boat up to the bridge. A drunken watchman standing guard over the area ordered the fisherman to leave. The fisherman refused so the guard grabbed an oar and started after the fisherman who then, in turn, brandished his boat hook. That apparently scared off the watchman—temporarily. He returned with a gun and started shooting, bullets flying everywhere, until an eyewitness subdued the guard and restored peace.

During the mid-1920s a number of movies were shot on the beach and the film industry was instrumental keeping up repairs on the dilapidated bridge. In 1926 caravans of camels and horses passed over the bridge for the filming of "The Son of the Sheik" staring Rudolf Valentino and Vilma Banky.

The few subsequent wooden bridges built to varying degrees of stability over the years were all destroyed by winter ice floes. The last bridge was washed away in 1927 and no new bridges were constructed for another 32 years.

TANGIER BRIDGE AT SMITH POINT AFTER IT
COLLAPSED IN 1927.
Photo courtesy of www.spoonercentral.com and the John Jett Collection

There was a Congressional hearing to try and find
out what happened to all the money invested by "Q" that
was lost, but nothing was determined, no one was charged,
and "Q" magically disappeared into the dried, yellow pages
of history never to be heard from again.

Walter T. Shirley came along some fifty years later
and managed to bring some of "Q's" plans to fruition.
Though today's street names in Mastic/Shirley area are
those as originally laid out by "Q's" surveyors and
architects, none refer to "Q", but one of the towns does
bears Shirley's name.

On July 4, 1959, after four years of construction, the
present day Smith Point Bridge opened. It is a 1200 foot
long draw bridge built on concrete pilings with a reinforced
concrete roadway laid on top of a steel beam superstructure
and cost $2.5 million dollars. It has a boat clearance of only
22 feet with a cranky old drawbridge that takes forever to
open and close delaying traffic in both directions.

Today, sixty years later, the old bridge needs to be retired and a replacement bridge erected. On June 11, 2019 The Suffolk County Legislature approved $73 million dollars in funding for a new bridge with the federal government picking up most of the cost.

Construction is scheduled to begin in 2021 and should take two years to complete. It will be 55 ft. above the high water mark providing enough clearance for most boats to pass beneath. The new bridge is expected to have a 75 to 100 year life span to accommodate the million visitors who come to Smith Point Park each year.

A RENDERING OF THE NEWLY PROPOSED SMITH POINT BRIDGE SCHEDULED TO BE COMPLETED IN 2023.
Photo courtesy of Suffolk County Public Works.

Let's hope that the ghosts haunting the Tangier Bridge have all fled along with "Q" and the new bridge serves us safely and efficiently as promised.

Thanks to Ken Spooner, and his amazing website www.spooner.com *for much of the information contained in this article. Check it out. You will not be disappointed. It is filled with a wealth of information about Mastic/Shirley history.*

DEATH'S COLD HAND ON BOARD THE *LOUIS V. PLACE*

The crew was already exhausted, chilled down to their very bones after four days exposure to freezing cold rain and little sleep as the *Louis V. Place* approached New York harbor, Friday morning, February 8, 1895 with the weather worsening.

For the entire voyage from Baltimore to New York for the three-masted schooner carrying 1100 tons of coal had endured heavy weather. Its sails, rigging and hull were icing over. The crew reefed the upper sails after violent winds shifted to the NNE.

About 2 AM the winds shifted west with even greater fury setting up a dangerous cross sea. The constant snow and salt spray froze layer after layer of ice on the vessel. The added weight on the topside shrouds threatened its stability. By 7 AM her running rigging was frozen in their blocks, the sails stiff with ice, the decks sheeted with it, visibility near zero.

Captain William H. Squires ordered the crew to cut the halyards to douse the sails but the sails were frozen stiff and would not come down. He next tried to anchor the vessel in hopes of riding out the gale. He ordered the anchors let go, but they were imprisoned by the ice.

The *Louis V. Place*, now little more than a "drifting iceberg," broached sideway to the seas. The Captain dispensed bracing portions of grog to the crew advising them to don all their heavy weather gear in preparation for whatever fate had in store.

THE *LOUIS V. PLACE* SHROUDED IN ICE OFF THE
COAST OF FIRE ISLAND IN 1895.
Public Domain

Early the next morning a cresting wave lifted the
vessel and with a death blow cast her onto a sandbar. She
bumped a few times and then settled with a deep shudder,
approximately 300-400 yards off shore, just east of the
Lone Hill Fire Island Life Saving Station.

Listing heavily to port, seas sweeping her decks the
crew faced the choice of drowning or exposure. The
Captain and the crew scrambled up the rigging. The snow
and sea spray layered them with coat after coat of ice as
they struggled to lash themselves to the rigging.
Hypothermia quickly overtook them, hands, arms and legs
numb from the bitter cold. They had to force open their
eyes, their mouths, by conscious acts of will

Hypothermia occurs when the body temperature
falls below 95 degrees Fahrenheit usually from exposure to
extreme cold, especially in wet and windy conditions. The
body starts to shiver and the fingers begin to lose dexterity.
Drowsiness and mental confusion quickly follow making a
dangerous situation worse. Further exposure causes speech

58

to slur accompanied with the loss of motor skills. With temperatures approaching freezing death can occur in as little as 15 minutes.

Despite the snow and sand being blowing into his eyes by the gale force winds, surfman Fred Saunders, U.S.L.S.S. saw the *Louis V. Place* get tossed onto the bar. He immediately contacted both his Life Saving Station at Lone Hill and the one at Blue Point for assistance and soon crews of surfmen assembled on the beach with a surfboat and all the gear necessary for rigging a breeches buoy rescue—a Lyle gun to fire lines to the ship, and the pulley system attached to a life ring to haul those in danger to shore.

It was still snowing, the wind gusting between 50 to 70 mph creating a wind chill of minus 30 degrees Fahrenheit. At high tide 20 foot seas broke up onto the beach. "Porridge" ice cakes up to 2 feet thick ground against each other in the churning seas. Isolated towers of ice cakes six to eight feet high spotted the beach. It was impossible to launch a lifeboat.

Within hours Captain Squires was the first to die, his frozen body rattled down the ratlines as he fell, his body immediately swept out to sea. The ship's cook, Charlie Morrison from Brooklyn, was next, falling soundless, head first into the seas. Just before dark, the engineer, Charles Allen fell backwards, arms outstretched Christ-like. He was followed shortly thereafter by the 200 lb. crewman, Lars Givby. The handsome, young blonde Norwegian Fritz Ward froze to death that same night, hanging head down in the rigging, held aloft by his lashings, lurching back and forth in the cold gale winds. Death's cold hand gripped the *Louis V. Place.*

Soren Nelson and Claus Stuven fashioned a shelter of sorts by cutting away the lines furling the mizzen topsail and crawling inside the folds of the sail. Seaman August Olsen, 28 years old, attempted to join them but he was below the crosstree and unable to climb up to their shelter despite attempts to help him. He died that night, frozen to the rigging like a human icicle.

WRECK OF THE SCHOONER *LOUIS V. PLACE*
Public Domain

Between snow squalls, when visibility availed, the surfmen fired numerous lines out to the stranded ship trying to effectuate a breeches buoy rescue. When one line fell close, Claus Stuven clambered down to the deck, numb-clumsy with hypothermia. He took hold of the line and pulled but the ice-caked rope was too heavy and he had to drop it. There was no way a breeches buoy rescue could work. With the survivors in extremis the surfmen needed to launch a lifeboat.

Finally, near midnight, Saturday, 40 hours after the *Louis V. Place* had run aground, the weather abated enough for the surfmen to launch a lifeboat into the seas still running high and choked with ice. A crew of seven—six on oars, one on sweep—rowed out through the maelstrom, growlers of ice pounding against the hull mercifully making their way alongside the doomed hulk.

LAUNCHING A SURFBOAT TO THE RESCUE
Courtesy of NPS.gov

Upon hearing their rescuers calling for them, the two survivors slowly made their way down the rigging hand over hand, boots slipping on the icy ratlines, and stumbled into the rescue arms of the boat crew. They were immediately rowed ashore into the capable hands of Dr. George Robinson of Sayville.

The rescuers cut the boots off the frozen feet of the survivors, dressed them in warm, dry clothing, rubbing their extremities trying to get their blood circulating. The stricken sailors were transported to a marine hospital on Staten Island where Nelson died a few days later. Stuven recovered and returned to sea but, it was said, he was never again the same. He took to selling postcards of himself, door to door.

61

Meanwhile, a crowd of a thousand spectators braved the weather, sleighing across the frozen bay to the beach to witness the spectacle. They came in such numbers that a roadway through the fallen snow was clearly visible over the frozen bay from Bayport to Lone Hill.

Someone got hold of Nelson's and Stuven's boots, cut them into pieces and distributed them as souvenirs.

On Sunday another surfboat was launched and the surfmen retrieved the remaining dead bodies, cutting them, still frozen, from the rigging. The bodies were transport to the mainland for proper burial.

Several days later he body of Captain Squires washed ashore some 30 miles to the east, opposite his birth place in Good Ground (Hampton Bays). He was buried in the local family plot.

Lars Givby's body was found near Forge River, Moriches, still clutching a length of line from the ship in a death grip. He was buried, with the line in his hand, alongside Fitz Ward and August Olsen—three bodies, two coffins, one large grave in a donated plot in Patchogue.

The body of Charles Morrison, the ship's cook from Brooklyn, was never found but tales abound about a lone ghost wandering Fire Island's dunes.

The keeper of the Lone Hill LSS, Sim Baker, remained on the beach for the duration of the rescue mission, his hands and feet sustaining severe frostbite. He contracted double pneumonia and later died. The crews from both stations also suffered from acute frostbite and exposure.

The ship itself broke up completely within a few weeks. The village of Patchogue purchased one of the masts and erected it as a flagpole.

From the sixth through the ninth of February 1895, the surfmen of the USLSS on Fire Island tended to a total of 29 vessels that had experienced storm and/or sea related disasters including the *John B. Manning* that had run aground off Fire Island shortly before the *Louis V. Place*, about one mile further east. All told, the life-saving servicemen rescued 129 crew members, and, with the exception of the *Louis V. Place*, without a single loss of life.

The Surfman's Motto back then was, "You have to go out to sea, but you don't have to come back."

O WHITMAN! MY WHITMAN!

Walt Whitman, born some 200 years ago, March 31, 1819. 'Tis of thee we sing celebrating your birth!
"Starting from fish-shape Paumanok, where [you were] born, well-begotten, and rais'd by a perfect mother...isle of salty shore and breeze and brine."

Printer's Devil, typesetter, pressman, editor, publisher, teacher, writer, government clerk, nurse, poet of the exclamation point!

All of the above!

WALT WHITMAN
Public Domain

You wrote of yourself:

"Walt Whitman, an American, one of the roughs, a kosmos, disorderly, fleshly, and sensual, no sentimentalist, no stander above men or women or apart from them, no more modest than immodest."

Spanning transcendentalism to realism, founder of American poetry in a nation no older than a lone man's life span, singing the praises of exuberant, young America, Whitman was Democracy. "His compositions, at least; being like it, ignorant, sanguine, noisy, coarse, and chaotic!"

"I celebrate myself,
And what I assume you shall assume,
For every atom belonging to me, as good belongs to you."

LEAVES OF GRASS p45
Public Domain

Almost out of breath with exaltation, we sing a song of celebration! A book of poetry! *Leaves of Grass*, was born, fittingly, on the 4th of July, 1855, and went through nine revisions until its "Deathbed Edition," in 1891. Containing but 12 untitled poems within its first edition—a mere 795 copies published and paid for by Whitman—this future canon was generally ignored except for several reviews calling it "trashy, profane and obscene," and its author "a pretentious ass."

Ralph Waldo Emerson, the transcendentalist philosopher, on the other hand, wrote, "I find it the most extraordinary piece of wit and wisdom that America has yet contributed...I find incomparable things said incomparably well as they must be. I find the courage of treatment which so delights us, and which large perception only can inspire."

Ezra Pound, the expatriate American modernist poet, called Whitman, "America's poet...He is America." Biographer, editor, and critic, William Sloane Kennedy wrote, "people will be celebrating the birth of Walt Whitman as they are now the birth of Christ."

It should come as no surprise, then, that Whitman had *"not one a barleycorn less"* of appreciation for his own talent, sounding his barbaric YAWP to the beautiful and perfect multitudes. In *Leaves of Grass*, one poem, [reaching beyond 1300 lines, later appropriately titled "Song of Myself"] reads in part:

"Divine am I inside and out, and I make holy whatever I touch or am touched from; The scent of these arm-pits is aroma finer than prayer...I breathe the fragrance myself and know it and like it...while they

discuss I am silent, and go bathe and admire myself... nor am I contained between my hat and boots."

Confounded by the Civil War Whitman wrote, *"Beat! Beat! Drums!"* as a rallying cry for the North.

"Beat! beat! drums! Blow! bugles! blow! Through the windows—through the doors—burst like ruthless force...scatter the congregation...the bridegroom...the bride...the peaceful farmer...Beat! beat! drums!—Blow! bugles! blow..."

Whitman's sensitive nature, however, was profoundly affected by the Civil War. In his book *Memorandum of War* he described the horrors he came upon, "a heap of amputated feet, legs, arms, hands, &c., a full load for a one-horse cart." There were, he wrote, "human fragments, cut, bloody, black and blue, swelled and sickening. Nearby were several dead bodies…each cover'd with its brown woolen blanket."

INTERIOR HAREWOOD HOSPITAL, WASH. DC. 1864
https://commons.wikimedia.org/w/index.php?curid=43881600

The sight moved him to volunteer as a nurse. He helped surgeons with amputations, and assisted in the burial of bodies, still bloody, still lying out on battlefields. He then turned to console the wounded soldiers, soothe them, and write letters for them.

Chastened by the war, Whitman wrote less self-aggrandizing, some might say less self-conscious poetry. "Drum Taps," which he included in later editions of *Leaves of Grass* contains 43 poems.

"To the drum-taps prompt, the young men falling in and arming, the mechanics... blacksmiths... lawyer... judge... driver...salesman—the boss the bookeeper, porter all leaving, squads gather everywhere by common assent and arm...The tearful parting—the mother kisses her son—the son kisses mother. (Loth is the mother to part—yet not a word does she speak to detain him.)... (Silent cannons—soon unlimber'd to begin the red business.)"

Whitman lived an unconventional life. He never married and his affections for young men, whom he called "my darlings and gossips," continued throughout his life.

Whitman, the only passenger on a streetcar, met its conductor, Peter Doyle, one night. As Doyle later recalled, "We were familiar at once—I put my hand on his knee—we understood."

Before Doyle, there was Fred Vaughn, who may have inspired Whitman's "Calamus" poems. There were, as well, Bill Duckett and William Stafford. Stafford wrote to Whitman about a ring Whitman had given him, "You know when you put it on there was but one thing to part it from me, and that was death."

Whitman's "obscene" poetry and bohemian lifestyle continued to dog him. Shortly after the war, Whitman was fired from his job in the Interior Department because of his questionable "moral character." A long-time friend, William Douglas O'Connor, immediately came to Whitman's defense—at great risk to O'Connor's own career. O'Connor secured a position for Whitman in the Bureau of Indian Affairs, and published a vigorous defense of Whitman in a 46 page pamphlet, lauding his poetry, his hospital work, and his love of country. It was entitled *The Good Gray Poet*. The pamphlet's message transformed the "immoral" poet into the "good gray poet", an appellation that stuck with him for the rest of his life.

Whitman gained international fame in 1868 when William Michael Rossetti, a writer and critic, published *The Poems of Walt Whitman* in England. Rossetti demanded changes to some poems but Whitman objected: "I cannot and will not consent, of my own volition, to countenance an expurgated edition of my pieces." So, Rossetti merely eliminated any poems he thought his readers might find objectionable and published the rest.

In 1873 Whitman suffered a stroke, partially paralyzing his left side, forcing him to move in with his brother George, his mother, and his youngest brother, Edward. Three days later his beloved mother passed away casting Whitman into a deep depression.

Whitman was finally able, both physically and financially, to buy a home of his own in 1883, in Camden, N.J. While there he continued working diligently. He finished the final revision of *Leaves of Grass*, assembled the *Memorandum of War* from journal entries and notes, and wrote *Specimen Days,* as well as some lesser-known works.

WALT WHITMAN'S HOME, CAMDEN, N.J.
Public domain

Walt Whitman died in his Camden home on March 26, 1892 at the age of 73. Over a thousand visitors came to pay their last respects, his coffin barely visible beneath all the wreaths and flowers.

In his poem, "When Lilacs Last in the Dooryard Bloom'd" Whitman confronts death:

"Come lovely and soothing death,
Undulate round the world, serenely arriving, arriving,
In the day, in the night, to all, to each,
Sooner or later delicate death."

[Note] Italics indicate direct quotes from Whitman's poetry.

FIRE ISLAND HAS A SCHOOL!

Fire Island has a school! It's only school, the Woodhull School, is a public school located on the SE corner of Midway and Surf Rd. on the border of Ocean Beach in the Fire Island National Seashore. It is named after Richard Woodhull who served first as a teacher and then as principal from 1924 until his retirement in 1935. It currently serves between 20 to 30 students from Preschool through Grade 6.

Founded in 1918 by Mina A. Woodhull, Richard's mother, the school is over 100 years old. Like most things Fire Island, the school had a hardscrabble history from its earliest days when the kids were only schooled during the summer through historical storms and deprivations.

Mina Woodhull, founder of the school, taught out of a local house in Ocean Beach until 1924 when a one room schoolhouse was built.

In these early days there was no electricity of course. Most homes, including the schoolhouse, were heated by coal stoves firing boilers that produced steam for radiators. The village of Ocean Beach was lit by oil street lamps scattered about the village, enough to light the walkways for a few hours each night.

There was no running water back then either. Water was drawn daily from any one of the hand-pump wells situated about town. Many families had their personal favorite.

Possibly the most remarkable schoolmaster the school ever had was Mr. Erwin W. Claus who served as schoolmaster for eleven years from 1925 to 1936. He was both the teacher and the village lamplighter. He also taught Sunday school.

Claus lived at the school in a small front bedroom and was responsible for cleaning the school, washing the windows and blackboards. He also prepared lunch and snacks for each pupil.

Each day classes started with the Pledge of Allegiance, "My Country Tis of Thee," followed by "The Star Spangled Banner," prayers and Bible readings.

EDWIN W. CLAUS AND STUDENT KIPPY HOMS
Courtesy of Frank Mina

Claus' duties as official lamplighter made him a popular figure. Thin and stooped, he could be seen carrying his ladder from street to street, trimming wicks, and filling oil reservoirs. As needed he would paint each lamppost. It took him a week, maybe more, for him to complete the job.

Not all teachers were as loved as Mr. Claus. According to a *New York Daily News* article dated June 13, 1982, Lillian Whitlock (nee Smith), one of 12 children, was schooled here on the beach with the rest of her siblings by William Thompson, a NYC teacher who, according to Ms. Whitlock, was "as strict a school teacher as could be found." In anticipation of Thompson's arrival by boat each June, her aunt, Lillian Slatterley, remarked, "I'd just as soon see the devil come ashore."

SCHOOL HOUSE
Courtesy of fi.k12.ny.us

For a time, Fire Island had two schools in operation, the one in Ocean Beach and another in Kismet Park until the Kismet school was destroyed by the 1938 hurricane almost immediately after it was completed.

In 1954 the current school was constructed. A gymnasium was added in 1975 and the library, dedicated to Harold Wilder, in 1986. The Alexander M. Van DeMark wing, named after another long time teacher, principal and superintendent, was added in 1991.

These self-same Woodhulls who founded the school and dedicated so much of their lives to the education of the children of Fire Island boast a proud, but little known heritage, all their own. They are descendents of Abraham

Woodhull (October 7, 1750 –January 23, 1826), a lead member of the famous Culper spy ring which provided George Washington with invaluable secrets during the Revolutionary War.

Along with Benjamin Tallmadge, Robert Townsend and Caleb Brewster, they ran the spy ring from NYC, to Setauket, L.I., and Norwalk, Connecticut and were responsible for highly successful operations including uncovering Benedict Arnold as a traitor.

A familiar tale involves Anna Strong who aided the ring by hanging her black petticoat out to dry with a number of white kerchiefs indicating in which of six coves the courier spy would meet Woodhull.

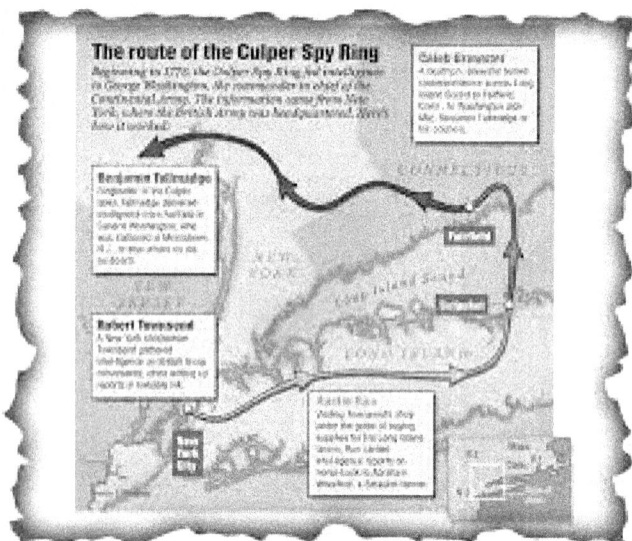

THE ROUTE OF THE CULPER SPY RING
Courtesy of the Three Village Historical Society

These stories can be seen on the docudrama entitled, "TURN: Washington's Spies."

The Mission Statement of the Woodhull school reads as follows: "The Fire Island School District believes in a collaborative approach to instruction that is designed to meet the individual needs of the students. Our mission is to create a safe, supportive, student-centered environment. We are committed to helping all children achieve academic excellence through creative challenges within our unique island setting. Our goal is to prepare the students to be dynamic citizens of our ever-changing society."

In pursuit of these goals the school offers programs in art, music, PE, Spanish and library skills, in addition to the usual three "Rs." Students attend grades from Pre-K to Grade 6, with free tuition for children of all residents. A limited number of off-island students are also welcomed but they are required to pay a nominal fee. Each student is provided with his/her own laptop computer, and that coupled with the low student-to-teacher ratio has resulted in high academic achievements.

Well done Woodhull school.

THE SHINNECOCK LIGHTHOUSE—
SOMETHING IS MISSING

Necessity builds lighthouses. Progress replaces them. Nostalgia preserves them.

At one point there were three proud lighthouses standing guard over the south shore of Long Island: Fire Island Lighthouse, Montauk Lighthouse, and Shinnecock Lighthouse. Today only two remain. Where the Shinnecock Lighthouse once stood, something is missing.

Even back in the mid 19th century something was missing. There was a 67-mile dark void between the Montauk Light and the Fire Island Light. In response to a query from the Lighthouse Board about the efficacy of their lighthouses, C.R. Mumford, commander of the packet-ship *Wisconsin*, wrote the following: "Within the last few years a great number of vessels have been stranded between Montauk Point light and Fire Island light; and in many instances there has been a great loss of life ... I would most respectfully suggest that a powerful flashing light be placed on some elevated position about halfway between Montauk and Fire Island lights."

In response, funds were appropriated for the Great West Bay Lighthouse and 10 acres of land were purchased on Ponquogue Point in the hamlet of Good Ground (as it was called back then). The location was selected, about one mile north of the beach, because the sand closer to the beach had been deemed too unstable.

Construction began in 1854. The lighthouse itself was a red brick tower, 168 feet high (with 178 steps) requiring 800,000 bricks to complete. Two keeper's homes were built on either side connected to the tower by covered walkways. On 1 January 1858 the Great West Bay Lighthouse was lit and that something that was missing was missing no more—only temporarily as it turned out.

The lighthouse station was more than just bricks and mortar. It was alive with families. The first keeper was named Charles A. Conley and his salary was $500 dollars/year. Over the years there were fifteen head keepers, fifteen first assistant keepers, and seventeen second assistant keepers, most from long-established local families, many with children.

SHINNECOCK LIGHTHOUSE WITH KEEPER BUILDINGS
Courtesy of USCG Lighthouse Friends
Craig Anderson

One of those children, Hope Penny, would dash all the way up those 178 steps into the loving arms of her father, Waldo Penny, the keeper, whenever she got in trouble with her mother.

Lucy and Alice Thomas, two young daughters of another keeper of the light, sent two dollars to Bishop Manning for construction of the Cathedral of St. John the

Divine in NYC. In the accompanying letter they wrote: "I am sending one dollar from my sister and one dollar from myself for completing the cathedral. We live at a lighthouse. My father is one of the keepers. We hope the cathedral will be a great light to all people who visit it, as our light here is to the ships at sea."

SHINNECOCK LIGHTHOUSE KEEPER WALDO PENNY
AND FAMILY CIRCA 1923
Courtesy of Richard Casabianca

This same Alice Thomas kept a memoir of a typical day at the lighthouse. "Work for the keepers was never ending. Each morning at 8 a.m., the three keepers assembled in the hallway and preceded up the tower, usually carrying a scuttle of coal, a 5-gallon can of kerosene or other supplies. The 'light' was a lantern fueled by kerosene, and the wick had to be trimmed and bottom filled [with fuel]. All glass and brass in the lantern room was polished daily."

Unfortunately, something else was missing way back in the mid 1800s, this time with deadly consequences. There were no *Notices to Mariners* back then to warn sailors of changes to navigational aids.

In late February 1858, the 203 foot, three-masted *John Milton* was ending a 15-month voyage unaware of the new lighthouse. Its captain mistook the Shinnecock Light for the Montauk Light, turned north and ran aground. All 33 aboard perished.

Changes continued over the years. The name of the lighthouse was changed to the Shinnecock Lighthouse in 1893 and the name Good Ground was changed to Hampton Bays in 1922. Numerous bird strikes required window replacements. (Edible fowl were harvested for dinner.) An oil house was added in 1890. In 1907 fuel for the light was changed from oil to oil vapor which tripled its luminescence. In 1915 the light characteristic was changed from a fixed white light to three white flashes every seven-and-a-half seconds.

In 1931, a red skeleton tower affixed with an electric light was erected on the beach near the Shinnecock Inlet to replace the lighthouse. On August 1, just after sunrise, the Shinnecock Lighthouse light was extinguished for the last time and the station was abandoned.

It showed its pedigree, ironically, when the 1938 hurricane destroyed that red skeleton tower while the Shinnecock Lighthouse stood tall and proud—but empty.

From 1931 until 1948 it stood neglected and forsaken, jilted by time. The Coast Guard offered to lease the light station to the Town of Southampton for one dollar a year, but the town refused. Local residents had the building inspected and it was found to be "safe and stable," but funds were lacking for its salvation.

GASOLINE SOAKED TIMBERS BURN, UNDERMINING
THE SHINNECOCK LIGHTHOUSE.
(Courtesy of USCG Lighthouse Friends Craig Anderson)

Three days before Christmas in 1948, demolition of the Shinnecock Lighthouse began. Bricks were removed from a section of the base of the tower and replaced with heavy timbers which were doused with gasoline and set afire. Shinnecock Lighthouse was alight one last time.

As the timbers burned away, the tower began to lean and then crashed onto the good ground with a dull thump heard miles away. It littered the earth with its 800,000 bricks.

TIMBER! THE SHINNECOCK LIGHTHOUSE FALLS.
Courtesy of USCG Lighthouse Friends Craig Anderson

A local newspaper reported the event as follows:

"There were tears in the eyes of many old timers who stood watching the old landmark pass away, powerless to save the old building. We did our best to save it, but in vain. Thus passes a landmark that will be missed by thousands ashore and by those who still used the old Ponquogue Lighthouse as a guide to bring them safely to land from the sea."

Something was missing.

And remained missing until, finally, on July 7, 2012 an historic marker was unveiled near where the lighthouse once stood. Richard Casabianca, whose great grandfather, Waldo Penny, had been one of the keepers of the light, was instrumental in erecting the marker. Mr. Casabianca remarked that the loss of the lighthouse was "final, hurtful, and wasteful. Imagine how our lives might be enriched if it were still standing."

He later added that the loss is "an ambiguous loss...leaving people shaking their heads in resignation and grief for decades, even by those who weren't there or even alive at the time. In other words, you can't quite get rid of something that isn't here anymore...Take the long view that sites and structures matter...Don't let politics, budgets, or fashion, or people in power right now, determine the death of anything so significant to past and future."

There may now be an historic marker in place of the old Shinnecock Lighthouse, but something is still missing.

I would like to thank the following people for providing me information necessary for writing this article: Eric Jay Dolin, Tom Perrin, Ken Mades, and, most especially, Richard Casabianca.

CELEBRATING JOHN MUIR: "FATHER OF THE NATIONAL PARKS"

It is fitting we celebrate John Muir, founder of the Sierra Club and the man righteously called the "Father of the National Parks."

John Muir (April 21, 1838 – December 24, 1914) is a well-known hero among environmentalist, but for those unfamiliar with his story here is a *too* brief summary.

John Muir was born in Dunbar, Scotland and immigrated to Wisconsin, U.S. with his family at the age of eleven. John had a curious, inventive mind and at the age of 22 he had devised several practical devices that he presented at the local state fair in Madison, devices that won prizes. Among his inventions were a horse feeder, a thermometer, and a gadget that tipped him out of bed in the morning.

John's father allowed him to get up at 1 AM to study if he so desired, to which John rhapsodized: "I had gained five hours, almost half a day! Five hours to myself! Five huge, solid hours! I can hardly think of any other event of my life, any discovery I ever made that gave birth to joy so transportingly glorious as the possession of these five frosty hours."

And study he did, his main interests being botany and geology, subjects he pursued his entire life.

"THE MOUNTAINS ARE CALLING ME AND I MUST GO."

In 1867 he suffered an eye injury that blinded him for about a month. Upon recovery he vowed to spend the rest of his days surrounded by nature and thus began his wanderlust. "This affliction has driven me to the sweet

87

fields. God has to nearly kill us sometimes, to teach us lessons."

He walked 1000 miles from Indianapolis to Cedar Key, FL "by the wildest, leafiest and least trodden way I could." He caught a boat to Cuba, Panama and, eventually, San Francisco. There he asked for the best way out of town.

"Where do you want to go?" he was asked.

"To any place that is wild," he replied.

And so it was that he found himself wading through waist high wild flowers in the San Joaquin Valley, into the high country of the Sierra Nevada Mountains. He wrote: "From this vast golden flower bed rose the mighty Sierra, miles in height, and so gloriously colored and so radiant, it seemed not clothed with light, but wholly composed of it, like the wall of some celestial city...the Sierra should be called the Range of Light." Muir found Yosemite. Muir found home.

JOHN MUIR
"John Muir National Historic Site" by National Park Service is licensed under CC BY 2.0

"IN EVERY WALK WITH NATURE ONE RECEIVES MORE THAN HE SEEKS."

Muir remained in the Sierra Nevadas for several years working as a shepherd, and guide. He also ran a sawmill. His intimate exposure to the wilderness convinced him that Yosemite Valley had been formed by glaciers and not by earthquakes as was the popular notion of the time. This brought him to the attention of many scholars, including one of his favorite authors, Ralph Waldo Emerson, who knocked on his log cabin door one day, and tried to induce Muir to go east and become a teacher. Muir, however, considered himself an unfinished student of nature and remained in the mountains, earning the sobriquet "John of the Mountains."

"HOW TERRIBLY DOWNRIGHT MUST BE THE UTTERANCES OF STORMS AND EARTHQUAKES TO THOSE ACCUSTOMED TO THE SOFT HYPOCRISIES OF SOCIETY."

Now and again he would leave the valley. He lived in San Francisco for a time writing a series of articles entitled *Studies in the Sierra* which launched his literary career. He would go on to write over 300 articles and 10 books. He continued travelling and made his first trip to Alaska during this time. He also married Louie Wanda Strentzel, had two daughters, and went in partnership with his father-in-law for ten years, managing their fruit farm with great success.

His wife encouraged his travels and he took several more trips to Alaska, as well as South America, Australia and even to the Far East. He would take his daughters on his "local" trips whenever possible. He once told a visitor to his farm, "This is a good place to be housed in during stormy weather...to write in, and to raise children in, but it is not my home. Up there," he said, pointing towards the Sierra Nevada range," is my home." The house and part of the farm are now designated as the John Muir National Historic Site.

"THESE TEMPLE DESTROYERS, DEVOTEES OF RAVAGING COMMERCIALISM, SEEM TO HAVE A PERFECT CONTEMPT FOR NATURE...LIFT THEIR EYES TO THE ALMIGHTY DOLLAR"

Yosemite Valley was threatened by "hoofed locusts" (Muir's derogatory name for sheep) alarming him of the danger of losing this pristine wilderness forever. He fell in with Robert Underwood Johnson, editor of *Century Magazine*, one of the most influential publications of its time. They were both of a mind to save Yosemite and a series of articles, written by Muir and published by Johnson, brought much needed attention to the problem.

In 1890 Congress created Yosemite National Park. Muir was also personally involved in the establishment of the Grand Canyon, Glacier, Sequoia, and Mount Rainier National Parks earning him the well-deserved title of the "Father of the National Parks."

PRESIDENT THEODORE ROOSEVELT AND JOHN MUIR
AT YOSEMITE 1904

Encouraged by Johnson, Muir went on to found The Sierra Club in 1892, based on the model of the Appalachian Mountain Club. He became its president and served as such until his death in 1914. The club's first major battle was the damming of Hetch Hetchy Valley to provide water for San Francisco, a debate between the preservationists and the conservationists. The Sierra Club lost, but the debate aroused public interest in the preservation of these wilderness areas and led to the creation of the National Park Service on August 25, 1916.

"A FAST AND A STORM AND A DIFFICULT CANON WERE JUST THE MEDICINE I NEEDED."

John Muir was strong and sinewy, 5'9" tall and never weighed more than 150 lbs. He travelled light. "I rolled up some bread and tea in a pair of blankets with some sugar and a tin cup and set off..." usually with a copy of Emerson.

On his many adventures he oftentimes risked his life seemingly without any concern for his personal safety. He loved storms and would venture out so that he could enjoy the grandeur of the fury. "When I heard the storm and looked out I made haste to join it; for many of Nature's finest lessons are to be found in her storms."

On one occasion he clung to the face of a precipice with no hope of reaching its top only to, somehow, do so. He purposely climbed to the top of a hundred-foot spruce in the middle of storm so that he could watch the wind. In Alaska he left camp with a dog called Skiteen in the middle of a blizzard just to go exploring. He was gone for some 16 hours, at one point forced to bridge a glacial crevasse on a narrow sliver of ice. Somehow he, or rather he and Skiteen, survived all these travails—and others.

"NO AMOUNT OF WORD-MAKING WILL EVER MAKE A SINGLE SOUL TO 'KNOW' THESE

91

MOUNTAINS. ONE DAY'S EXPOSURE TO MOUNTAINS IS BETTER THAN A CARTLOAD OF BOOKS."

While Muir is well known for these many exploits, he is little known for the facility of his writing—prose that approaches poetry. Take this example of his description of a storm on Mount Shasta:

"About half past 1 o'clock P.M. thin fibrous cloud films began to blow directly over the summit of the cone from north to south, drawn out in long fairy webs, like carded wool, forming and dissolving as if by magic. The wind twisted them into ringlets and whirled them in a succession of graceful convolutions, like the outside sprays of Yosemite falls; then sailing out in the pure azure over the precipitous brink of the cone, they were drifted together in light gray rolls, like foam wreaths on a river."

And take this description of his view from the top of that hundred-foot spruce he climbed in the middle of a storm:

"There is always something deeply exciting, not only in the sounds of winds in the woods, which exert more or less influence over every mind, but in their varied waterlike flow as manifested by the movements of the trees, especially those of the conifers. By no other trees are they rendered so extensively and impressively visible, not even by the lordly tropic palms or tree-ferns responsive to the gentlest breeze. The waving of a forest of the giant Sequoias is indescribably impressive and sublime, but the pines seem to me the best interpreters of winds. They are mighty waving goldenrods, ever in tune, singing and writing wind-music all their long century lives. Little,

however, of this noble tree-waving and tree-music will you see or hear in the strictly alpine portion of the forests."

John Muir died of pneumonia in Los Angeles at the age of 76 during a brief visit to his daughter. He was survived by his two daughters and ten grandchildren.

STATUE OF JOHN MUIR AS A YOUNG BOY
EDINBURGH, SCOTLAND
Public Domain

Scotland, the land of his birth, commemorates his birthday with John Muir Day. They have also named a 130 mile route *John Muir Way* in his honor.

The Muir Woods National Monument, Muir Beach, John Muir College, Mount Muir and Muir Glacier are all named in his honor among many, many more. The list goes on. He has a butterfly, a pika, a millipede, a wren, two species of aster, a rose, and even a mineral named after him.

He might find fault, however, with one name in particular—the 211 mile John Muir Hiking Trail in the Sierra Nevada Mountains. He would find no fault in the trail itself which he would love, but would have disliked its name.

"Hiking –" he wrote, *"I don't like either the word or the thing. People ought to saunter in the woods – not hike! Do you know the origin of that word 'saunter?' It's a beautiful word. Away back in the Middle Ages people used to go on pilgrimages to the Holy Land, and when people in the villages through which they passed asked where they were going, they would reply, 'a la sainte terre,' to the Holy Land. And so they became known as sainte-terre-ers or saunterers. Now these mountains are our Holy Land, we ought to saunter through them reverently, not 'hike' through them."*

God Bless you John Muir.

FREE UNION CHURCH OF OCEAN BEACH CELEBRATES ITS ANNIVERSARY

VINTAGE POSTCARD OF THE FREE UNION CHURCH
Courtesy of the Free Union Church

THE FREE UNION CHURCH located at Ocean Breeze Walk and Midway in Ocean Beach is over 100 years old, the oldest church on Fire Island. It is built of wood with high ceilings and fitted with beautiful stained glass windows donated by its parishioners.

For decades the church had been called the Union Free Church, but in 1998 workers discovered the original cornerstone revealing that the church's actual name was the Free Union Church. The trustees subsequently voted to restore the original name.

A commemorative book was issued on its centennial anniversary including a dedication from the trustees, a letter from the president of the trustees, and a letter from the mayor.

The majority of the book covers the history of the church. Subjects covered include the establishment of the church, facsimiles of important church documents, a list of all 42 past and present trustees, the charitable giving of the church over the years, AA involvement, gifts to the church, and last, but not least, color photos of the church's stained glass windows.

Aha! The inside story of the Free Union Church

The history of the Free Union Church goes all the way back to the founding of Ocean Beach. In 1908 a real estate speculator by the name of John A. Wilbur purchased a tract of land that now encompasses Ocean Beach. He subdivided the land into 25×100-foot lots, and offered them for sale for $100 apiece in various Brooklyn newspapers.

During the early years of Ocean Beach, religious services were held in the home of S. Nelson Irwin, MD and his wife. Wilbur, the speculator, was often present at these services. At one such service, Wilbur assured Irwin, his wife and sister-in-law, one Miss M. Louise Harper, that he would set aside a parcel of land for a church in Ocean Beach.

Like a dog with a bone, Miss M. Louise Harper would not let Wilbur forget his promise. Finally, after listening to Harper's constant reminders, Wilbur asked her to provide a document listing the names of those willing to pledge financial support for the church and the amounts they would guarantee.

On Nov. 15, 1915, Harper did so, showing a total commitment of $642.43 from eight signatories – including some monies that had already been deposited in the bank.

Wilbur then deeded the lots on which the church was eventually built to the church organization.

Most of the trustees lived in New York City at the time, but they journeyed to Ocean Beach in the middle of the winter of 1916 and on Feb. 25 of that year they legally established the church with the state.

Still, it took over a year before ground was broken and in the autumn of 1917 the cornerstone was laid. The architect was Frederick L. Wagner and the builder Anton Severin.

For her efforts Harper was designated as the church founder, and presented with a suitably inscribed pin. Work proceeded until the Free Union Church was completed and dedicated on Sunday, Aug. 25, 1918. In the fall of 1920 a special service was held to celebrate paying off the mortgage. It was quite appropriate that the burning paper was held between the delicate fingers of none other than Miss M. Louise Harper.

Interdenominational services are held from 10:45-11:30 a.m. each Sunday from Father's Day through Labor Day. Ministers of various denominations come to the island each week to preach to an average of 35 worshippers. Many ministers are provided by the True North Community Church of Bohemia. The church also houses meetings of the local AA chapter. Its main source of income is the annual Raffle and Cake Sale. Its board of trustees meets three times a year.

SALTAIRE IS 100 YEARS OLD

SALTAIRE?

The name Saltaire has a surprising origin. It is not, as many might assume, derived from some "olde English" spelling of the clean, fresh breath of God one inhales on Fire Island. Rather, it comes from an English town on the River Aire named after Lord Titus Salt, a successful textile entrepreneur.

Sir Titus Salt 1803-1876

The combination of quality housing for his employees, along with recreation, education, and social services was one of the first examples of modern urban planning. Salt's endeavor—at one time containing the largest industrial building in the world—was so successful that the English town Saltaire has been designated as a UNESCO World Heritage Site. So the powers-that-be decided it would be an apt choice for the name of their town but why someone came up with that name remains unknown to this day. Maybe it did have something to do with salt air.

BUT IN FIRE ISLAND'S SALTAIRE...

The infamous "Long Island Express" (the hurricane of 1938) cut a channel across Fire Island, from ocean to bay, killing 6 people, and devastated Saltaire. Of the 168 buildings at the time of the hurricane, only 20 remained unscathed. Eighty-nine buildings were completely destroyed, and four miles of boardwalk, including the Bay Promenade, were washed away.

Part of the reason for the extent of the damage was the Fire Island Beach Development Corporation's decision to bulldoze the dunes for better views of the ocean, eliminating them as protection from ocean waves.

However, true grit prevailed and by 1965 the community had recovered—recovered to such an extent that new zoning laws had to be enacted limiting the number of homes to 470.

HEROES?

One individual responsible for Saltaire's success was an Irish immigrant by the name of Michael Coffey. He originally worked as a carpenter for the Beach

Development Corporation before going out on his own. He built homes, as well numerous other buildings, from 1913 through 1950. These homes are called "Coffey Cottages" to this day. They were designed to utilize the cool prevailing breezes utilizing crown windows. His talents were soon in high demand.

MICHAEL COFFEY (1888-1963) FROM GALWAY, IRELAND, SALTAIRE'S MASTER BUILDER
Photo compliments of Bill Weinland

Michael met his future wife, Josephine, when he saw her walking down Saltaire's dock. For Michael it was love at first sight. They married in 1921 and raised their extended family in Saltaire. Josie was rumored to be quite a cook!

Coffey is rumored to have saved at least two women during the '38 hurricane. He built over 100 homes, the Saltaire Village Hall, and three churches (Our Lady of the Star—a second time after it was destroyed by the '38 hurricane). He also built the addition to the yacht club. After the hurricane he was instrumental in rebuilding Saltaire and continued to build, renovate and maintain homes until his death in 1963. His daughter, Anne Coffey Keegan, grandchildren, and great grandchildren are still involved in the Saltaire community.

There are many such stories about Saltaire and its inhabitants, some so sentimental that the story tellers are reluctant to share them—stories about times before electricity, or running water, the difficulties of getting children educated, dogsled rides over the frozen bay in winter—stories only for loved ones, not for publication. Alas, the loss...

AND THE YACHT CLUB?

The Saltaire Yacht Club had to be rebuild after extensive damage caused by yet another hurricane. Superstorm Sandy roared ashore in 2012. The yacht club sports tennis courts, the only restaurant/bar in town, and owns a fleet of boats offering sailing lessons to both children and adults. Its bar and restaurant hosts comedians, Broadway entertainers and singers. It also shows kids movies once a week. It also welcomes the children's Labor Day show.

SALTAIRE BOAT BASIN
Mrshllmx at Wikipedia, CC BY-SA 3.0

The Saltaire Volunteer Fire Company was established in 1969 and in 1986 it became the first Fire Island fire department to provide Emergency Medical Services (EMS) not only to Saltaire but to the neighboring communities as well. Because of their use in the unique Fire Island environment the two pumpers, two EMS first response vehicles, a rescue truck, and an ambulance, have all been modified with four wheel drive, lifted suspensions, and over-sized tires. These brave volunteers continue their heroic work to this day.

The village has restored the Bay Promenade as a boardwalk just as it was in 1912—and they have the photos to prove it.

Back in 2017 the Village of Saltaire celebrated its Centennial, 100 years since incorporation. The day-long festivities included:

- A Historical display in the Village Hall - first floor.
- Jim O'Hare, author of the Saltaire38.blogspot.com, presented a lecture "Saltaire History 102," covering the history of Saltaire from pre-Saltaire Fire Island through the present day.
- A reception with entertainers was held at the Saltaire Market deck.
- A Children's Pie Eating Contest in the style of the 1950s and 1960s.
- An evening concert at the ball field
- Two iMovies, produced by residents Brad Brown and Tracy Dockray covering the first fifty years, followed by the second half.

- A Centennial Party from 7:30 pm – 9:30 pm

TIME CAPSULE?

A Centennial Time Capsule was assembled by the Saltaire Citizens Association and then buried in the walls of the Village Hall as a message to future generations. In order to get the widest possible participation, block captains asked Saltairians to submit documents, photos, stories, and/or their favorite beach memories. Each walk contributed to the capsule.

Saltaire descendants will excavate it (or dive to it, if water levels rise as predicted) in 2050 for their amusement at the quaintness of their ancestors—and they may have cause for puzzlement as to why a raccoon was included.

THE MIRACULOUS RESCUE OF THE U.S.S. *NORTHERN PACIFIC*

THE U.S.S. *NORTHERN PACIFIC* AGROUND OFF
FIRE ISLAND JANUARY 1919.
Courtesy of the National Archives and Records Administration

No one knows how many wrecks have occurred off Fire Island's shores, some horrific (*Louis V. Place*), some forgotten by history, but the most miraculous rescue may be that of the U.S.S. *Northern Pacific* which ran aground on New Year's Day in 1919 with a shipload of wounded soldiers aboard.

The World War I troop carrier, the *U.S.S. Northern Pacific*, left Brest, France enroute to Hoboken, N.J. on Christmas Day 1918. On board were over 2500 Doughboys returning from WW I. Of those, more than 1500 were wounded—300 bedridden—with seventeen Navy nurses in attendance. Designed to carry 856 passengers and a crew of 198, the *Northern Pacific* was putting more than two and a half times that many individuals in jeopardy on that fateful voyage.

The ship approached the port of New York on Wednesday, New Year's Day, January 1, 1919, experiencing pouring rain and winds howling out of the southwest. It was foggy and the temperature was a chilling 45 degrees. Monstrous Atlantic Ocean waves pummeled the *Northern Pacific*, breaking over her superstructure and twin smokestacks. She was in trouble, and ran aground at 2:20 a.m. on a sand bar approximately 200 yards south of Fire Island. Immediately, attempts were made to back her off the bar, but they proved unsuccessful.

The ship's master, Captain L. Connelly, USN, promptly sent out an SOS. He was in constant contact by wireless with Captain B.W. Blamer, chief of staff to Admiral Gleaves, coordinator of rescue efforts. Despite the grave conditions, Captain Connelly sent a message to reassure the relatives of the returning servicemen that "they need have no fear for their safety."

Early that morning, a surfman, Roger Smith, sighted the ship a few miles southeast of Fire Island Life Saving Station #84 in Ocean Bay Park.

Soon a contingent of LSS surfmen was on scene firing breeches buoy lines out to the stricken vessel in attempts to affect a rescue. Heavy winds and high seas, however, prevented the shot lines from reaching the ship.

Alerted by the SOS, and with deadly concern for the catastrophic disaster facing the wounded men and their caretakers, numerous vessels immediately made for Fire Island, including the salvage tug *Resolute*, the cruisers *Columbia* and *Des Moines*, the transport *Henry R. Mallory*, six submarine chasers, and a minesweeper among others. Throughout the night they kept the *Northern Pacific* illuminated with their searchlights. The hospital ship *Solace* lay offshore ready to accept casualties should weather permit.

The local residents also pitched in to help. A fleet of small boats, both commercial and privately owned, gathered in Bay Shore, Long Island, ready to transport the stranded victims from the Fire Island beach, across 5 miles of the Great South Bay, to a steam locomotive ready to rush the wounded to hospital.

Storm warnings issued Wednesday morning by the U.S. Weather Bureau called for high intensity storms extending from Florida to Maine. The storms were moving eastward from the Great Lakes with turbulent southerly winds predicted to shift to the west the following day.

The winds increased throughout the night. One rogue wave swept down the side of the *Northern Pacific* tearing away a lifeboat from high on her superstructure. The ship was driven further on shore by the wild winds and violent seas, twisting her broadside into the sand bar where she came hard aground, listing heavily to her port side, in waters only 10 feet deep. An attempt to tow the 8,000 ton, 524 foot long *Northern Pacific* off the sand bar during high tide the following morning failed.

Thirty hours after the *Northern Pacific* ran aground the surfmen were finally able fire a line to the *Northern Pacific* and began rescue efforts using a breeches buoy apparatus. The line was secured from the ship to the shore where it was anchored to a tripod buried deep in the sand. The line carried a life ring attached to a pulley system, a scheme honed by decades of experience, but one only for the able and the desperate.

BREECHES BUOY USED TO RESCUE PASSENGERS
FROM THE U.S.S. *NORTHERN PACIFIC*.
Courtesy of the National Archives and Records Administration

Surfboats began ferrying the wounded, ten at a time, through the rough breakers to the shore. Rescues continued throughout the day and, in spite of the bitter cold and difficult sea conditions, 254 passengers including all seventeen nurses were successfully saved. The only casualty was a rescue motor launch from the cruiser *Columbia* which was swamped and driven ashore. The three men aboard were plucked from the icy waters and resuscitated by surfmen on the scene.

The weather abated somewhat, Friday, January 3rd enabling the rescue of an additional 210 troops. Numerous barrels of oil were spread on the seas in an attempt to calm them. Conditions, however, remained too hazardous to remove those most desperately needing saving—those on stretchers.

As the weather continued to improve, the submarine chasers with their shallow drafts and high maneuverability were finally able to approach the *Northern Pacific*'s leeward side and began disembarking the most severely wounded to the hospital ship *Solace*, and the ambulatory to the *Mallory* and other nearby ships. By noon on the Saturday, January 4th the last of the wounded men had been safely evacuated.

SURFBOATS OF THE U.S. LIFE SAVING SERVICE
MAKING WAY OUT TO THE U.S.S. *NORTHERN PACIFIC* TO
RESCUE THE STRANDED SOLDIERS.
Courtesy of the National Archives and Records Administration

After three and a half days of intense efforts everyone was saved. The experienced rescuers had proceeded deliberately, with patience and due caution, and, miraculously, there were no major injuries and not a single life was lost.

With all the troops safely removed, efforts turned to refloating the *Northern Pacific*. Barges and lighters came alongside and, using their powerful winches, removed the *Northern Pacific's* guns, her lifeboats and signal towers—anything heavy—to lighten the load. Three tugs fastened to her stern and pulled the ship seaward at each successive high tide. Progress was slow—gain a few feet, lose some. She was finally broken free of the sand bar and refloated on the evening of January 18th, two and a half weeks after her initial grounding. The surfmen of the Coast Guard maintained a continuous vigil during the ordeal.

Repairs to her damaged bottom plates and rudder required five months work before the *Northern Pacific* could return to duty. Subsequently, she made two more trans-Atlantic voyages.

Three years later, in February of 1922, while being towed to a shipyard in Pennsylvania, the *Northern Pacific* caught fire, capsized and sank in 150 feet of water, 30 miles south of Cape May, New Jersey where she remains, to this day, a favorite haunt of wreck divers.

RUMRUNNERS OF FIRE ISLAND

It all started with Prohibition.

Thanks to the active political participation of the Woman's Christian Temperance Union (WCTU), the Anti-Saloon League, and the likes of Carry A. Nation, an uncorseted woman ("bad for the vital organs" she claimed) who went about town with her handy hatchet chopping up taverns preaching "Death to Rum," in January 1919 the eighteenth amendment to the U.S. Constitution was ratified.

CARRY A. NATION WITH HER HATCHET AND HER BIBLE
Public Domain

NO MORE RUM!

Or gin either for that matter. Oh no, no whiskey or intoxicating spirits of any kind. Oh, oh, oh...NO MORE RUM!

This was quickly followed by the Volstead Act which set forth enforcement measures. President Woodrow Wilson vetoed the bill, but both the Senate and the House of Representatives overrode his veto and Prohibition became the law of the land, outlawing the manufacture, transportation, importation, exportation, and sale of intoxicating liquors.

But the "drys," as those supporting Prohibition were called, had greatly underestimated the public's thirst for alcohol. Parched throats needed slaking—even Presidents'! Both President Wilson and his successor, President Harding secreted their own personal liquor supplies in the White House and their personal residences.

It did not take long for boot-legging to turn America into a nation of "honest lawbreakers". The term "boot-legging", it is suggested, originated during the Civil War when soldiers would sneak liquor into camp in their boots. Civilians quickly took up the practice, hiding flasks in boots or trouser legs. The term stuck and came to include "rumrunners"—smugglers waiting offshore with their illicit swag.

With Prohibition, Fire Island awoke to a new reality. It lay close to New York City, the biggest market for this new, illegal contraband. With its long stretches of beaches, sparse population, ideal topography, and numerous inlets—in particular the relatively safe Fire Island Inlet, Fire Island became an ideal location for smugglers just as it had been for the pirates of yore.

Depending on which history book you read, either Bill "The Real" McCoy or William "Big Bill" Dwyer came up with concept of Rum-Row, a flotilla of large vessels (mother ships) stationed three miles off-shore in international waters. They would sell their illegal spirits to smaller, faster boats for transport to trucks waiting to take the hooch to market.

Bill McCoy was eventually captured by the Coast Guard after a fire fight with the cutter *Seneca*. Bill swore he was in international waters but pled guilty and served nine months in jail. He later retired to Florida, investing in real estate with his ill-gotten gains. The term "the real McCoy" comes from the fact (?) that Bill McCoy was famous for not diluting the booze he was selling. It was the real McCoy.

William "The Real" McCoy
Public Domain

Charley Byron, a Fire Island original, recounted a story about taking his grandfather's boat out the inlet to Rum-Row. He bought cases of liquor from an old Scottish rust bucket and took the booze directly to NYC where the police had conveniently segregated an area for offloading contraband. An undertaker drove it away in his hearse.

The Coast Guard soon instituted regular patrols in the Fire Island inlet to help curtail the smuggling. In response, those local fishermen, clam diggers, baymen, and small boat captains who had adopted this new lucrative trade needed alternative solutions. They would beach their boats through the surf and would then either bury the cases of liquor in the sand for later retrieval, or haul them across the island to the Great South Bay for quick runs to Long Island's south shore.

The New York Times reported that Islip was the destination for large quantities of alcohol. *The Suffolk County News* reported that two vessels, the *Columbia* and the *Maud Muller* had dropped off cases of liquor in West Sayville on the very day that the police were (conveniently) out of town helping to quell a strike in Buffalo. An ice house for storing fish near the Zee Line ferry terminal in Bay Shore was converted to a store house for liquor. Soon trucks were transporting ice dripping fish covered cases of booze into the city.

The infamous hotel, the White House, in Water Island, once the destination for the socially elite (including President Teddy Roosevelt it has been rumored), had fallen on hard times after WWI. Prohibition gave it new life and it returned to its glory days as a speakeasy and gambling casino. Even sleepy Saltaire had its "Casino" which openly served liquor. One self-confessed bootlegger specified Long Cove, Lonelyville and Ocean Beach as the primary destinations for the majority of the illegal liquor.

Some of the more renowned speakeasies included the Canoe Place Inn (CPI), aka Tammany Hall East because of all the corrupt politicians who hung out there, and Claudio's of Greenport which still has a trap door behind the bar for access to illicit spirits floated in beneath the building.

Motor Parkway, originally built by William Vanderbilt as his own private raceway, found itself with nightly automobile races between the bootleggers and the police, a forerunner of what was to happen with moonshiners down south.

RUMRUNNER ON FIRE
Courtesy of U.S. Coast Guard

And so the game proceeded. In 1924, Congress extended U.S. territorial waters out to 12 miles offshore hoping to increase the difficulty for smuggling. Undeterred, the smugglers built bigger and faster vessels.

Though the original armada of boats transporting the alcohol had been a ragtag fleet of sailboats, fishing boats, and recreational watercraft, with so much money involved bootleggers were soon building sleek speedboats, some equipped with 400 hp Liberty V-12 liquid-cooled aircraft engines. Even the newest Coast Guard vessels could not catch them.

Several Fire Island ferry boats enjoyed exciting lives as rum runners before retiring to their more sedate occupations. Just about all the old-salt captains from the various Fire Island ferry lines claimed to have been rumrunners during Prohibition. The ferry *Running Wild* and many other boats plying the bay in the 50s and 60s had been ferrying illegal booze before they began ferrying passengers. The *Running Wild* still had patched-over 50 caliber machine gun bullet holes in its hull when it was sold to a gentleman from Sayville.

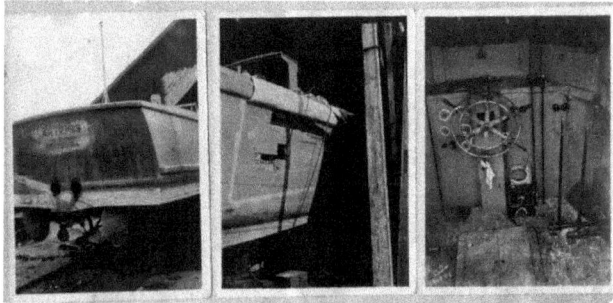

RUMRUNNER *ARTEMIS*, LATER THE FIRE ISLAND FERRY *SOUTH BAY COURIER*. SHE WAS ENGAGED IN A GUN BATTLE WITH USCG. AFTER BOOZE DELIVERY TO CLAUDIO'S IN GREENPORT
Courtesy of http://saltaire38.blogspot.com

The *Artemis* (later the Fire Island ferry boat *South Bay Courier*) was another. It was engaged in a gun battle with the Coast Guard after delivering booze to Claudio's. Snyd Zegel had the *Artemis* and her sister ship the *Margaret* (both built by the Wheeler Shipyard in Coney Island) outfitted with three Hall-Scott Invader engines. According to one story, Snyd had just loaded a hull-full of illegal booze when the Coast Guard ran up on him. He raced them all the way from the Fire Island inlet to Montauk and was never caught. He was later informed that the *Artemis* had been clocked at 42 knots.

The most successful tactic employed by the bootleggers however was bribery. Less than a year after Prohibition began a hundred NYC agents were fired for taking bribes. Corruption was rampant from the federal level, down to town officials, down to the local police. Even the Coast Guard was not immune. When the sloop *J.H.B.* ran aground off Point O' Woods, the CG pulled the boat off the sandbar only to discover it contained $75,000 dollars of illegal liquor. The boat's captain was taken ashore by the CG to make a phone call and inexplicably "escaped."

Back then a CG seaman earned just $30/week. A single run out to Rum-Row, a half-a-day's excursion, was worth $400 dollars (more than three months salary) making honesty a questionable virtue. When the Chief of the Fire Island CG station was away, his second-in-command called the authorities to inform them of the rampant bribery. Afterwards, he was threatened with arrest along with the guilty. He decided to remain silent.

With so much money in play, it did not take long for the Mafia to insert itself. Al Capone, nineteen at the time, earned his reputation running rum in Amityville. When he relocated to Chicago, Dutch Schultz, headquartered in Patchogue, took control of all area rum-running operations. In 1932, The *New York Evening Journal* reported that organized crime paid $1 million dollars in bribes to the Coast Guard to insure the safe delivery of their contraband. Honest surfmen were known to have been beaten and/or shot.

But the mood in the country was changing. The public became disenchanted with the results of Prohibition. The corruption was obvious. Crime was increasing. When bootleggers were caught red-handed some juries would fail to convict. Smuggling had become so efficient that the price of a case of liquor dropped from $6/case to $2 severely limiting profits. The advent of quality moonshine aggravated the situation.

CELEBRATING THE END OF PROHIBITION AT CLAUDIO'S
1933
"Courtesy of the Claudios Family & 'America in the 1930s' Facebook Group

Finally, on December 5, 1933 the Twenty-first Amendment to the Constitution was ratified and 13 years of Prohibition came to an end. While most of America celebrated, some clandestine operations failed, the White House Hotel at Water Island being one, but those 13 years provided ripe tales for Fire Islanders to recount (and, perhaps, embellish) to this day.

Cheers!

FORGOTTEN BAY SHORE AVIATION HISTORY

Long Island has a rich aviation history. It is home to the three busy airports serving NYC (JFK, LaGuardia, and MacArthur) as well as numerous small airports dotting the island that provide everything from recreational flying to flight training to sky diving. There are other significant airports that have been lost over time to shopping malls, schools, parks and suburban sprawl—Mitchel Air Force Base in Hempstead, Floyd Bennett Field in Brooklyn, and, of course, Roosevelt Field in Garden City, home to many famous aviation pioneers such as Amelia Earhart, Wiley Post and Charles Lindberg who took off from Roosevelt Field on that first celebrated transatlantic non-stop flight to Paris in 1927.

SEAWARD BOUND. U.S. AERO STATION, BAY SHORE, L.I. N.Y.

121

Aviation industry giants also claim Long Island as their places of birth. Republic Aviation in Farmingdale built the famous P-47 Thunderbolt, the most produced aircraft during WW II. The most famous has to be Grumman Aeronautical Engineering Company founded in 1930 by Leroy Grumman. The company started in Bethpage, moved to Calverton and grew into the largest employer on L.I., famous for its string of fighter planes, the Firecat, Hellcat, Tigercat and Bearcat that dominated the skies during WW II. Grumman continued its success with the A-6 Intruder in the 60s, the F-14 Tomcat in the 70s, as well as its fleet of Gulfstream executive jets. It is most famous for its Apollo project Lunar Excursion Module (LEM) that landed men on the moon in 1969.

But long before Grumman or Republic came along the little town of Bay Shore was giving birth to its own aviation pioneer. In 1915 Charles Lanier Lawrance moved to East Islip from Paris where he had studied architecture. Lawrance was an aeronautical engineer at heart and had developed an air-cooled, 200 hp engine that was revolutionary in an era when water-cooled engines were the standard. He also developed a new type of wing section with an exceptionally high lift-to-drag ratio.

Upon his return from Paris, Lawrance established the Bay Shore Air Club at the foot of Garner Lane, adjacent to Lawrence Creek in Bay Shore. The Air Club was for likeminded aviation enthusiasts excited by the invention of the airplane by the Wright brothers a mere 15 years earlier. In 1917 Lawrance founded the Lawrance Areo-Engine company and began manufacturing his revolutionary new air-cooled engines.

These engines were the direct ancestors of the famous Whirlwind engines renowned for their reliability, durability, and their endurance on extreme long-distance flights. They powered the planes of such famous aviators as Admiral Byrd, Amelia Earhart, and Charles Lindberg.

With the onset of World War I (1914-1918) the location of the Air Club was perfect for the Navy. It was strategically located, geographically close to New York City and its key sea lanes, and in close proximity to other aviation oriented facilities such as the Sperry Gyroscope Company in Brooklyn, the Curtis Aeroplane Company, and both Yale and MIT Universities which had begun turning out new Navy pilots. Thanks to Lawrance's Bay Shore Air Club, the site already had the beginnings of a naval air station.

HANGERS OF THE BAY SHORE NAVAL STATION AT GARNER LANE.

Lawrance leased the property to the U.S. Navy for $1 a year for the duration of the war making it the second naval base created in America after Pensacola, FL. In 1916 the Second battalion of the Naval Militia added eight acres to the base by dredging fill from the Great South Bay after which work began on the construction of five new hangers.

The purpose of the base was to train volunteers as pilots and aviation mechanics. At the peak of the war, the base was training approximately one thousand servicemen per day putting a logistical strain on the local communities. The Linwood Resort Hotel on South Clinton Ave, Bay Shore was used to house the airmen, but its facilities were outdated providing only limited heating during the winter. The Bay Shore Knights of Columbus held a fundraiser and purchased an old summer estate called Elysian View as additional accommodations for the troops. This site is now Saint Patrick's elementary school.

THE EAGLE BEATS THE SHARK. U.S. AERO STATION, BAY SHORE, L.I. N.Y.

Local luncheonettes did their best to feed the airmen. The Ladies of Bay Shore, led by the locals Mrs. Mulford and Mrs. Binkerhoff, fed lunch to 300 troops daily.

The Naval Base Bay Shore operated successfully throughout the entirety of the First World War. It was decommissioned in May 1919, and its personnel were transferred to Pensacola, FL. The remains of the base quickly disappeared. The growing population of the area put pressure on suburban development for housing. Prohibition and the prolific rum-running in the area immediately following the war did not help, and the coming of the Great Depression turned most minds to survival. No one thought to preserve the memory of the base as time moved on and its history has been all but forgotten.

Later in his life Charles Lawrance was asked that given the importance of his naval base and the immense success of pilots like Lindberg and Earhart who used his engines in their exploits why he remained relatively unknown. He replied, "Who remembers Paul Revere's horse."

Lawrence died in his East Islip home, Meadow Farm, in 1950.

The name of Paul Revere's horse was Brown Beauty.

Postcards from the heyday of the Bay Shore Naval Air Station reflect the drama and energy of early military aviation on Long Island. (From the collection of Long Island Maritime Museum)

PERSONAL STORIES OF THE HURRICANE OF 1938

AERIAL VIEW OF SALTAIRE TAKEN ON SEPT. 22, 1938
http://saltairian.com/pages/history/1938/pictures5.html

The hurricane hit Fire Island around 2:30 p.m., on Wednesday, 21 September 1938. The eye was about 50 miles wide, the storm itself about 500 miles across. High tide was even higher than usual because of the autumnal equinox when the sun and moon align with the Earth. Pushed by winds gusting over 180 mph, the sea surge, between 30 and 80 feet high (accounts vary), pounded the coastline with uncountable tons of seawater.

OCEAN BEACH/THE GREAT SOUTH BAY

"Let go the anchor!" Captain Harold Garrett bellowed over the howling gale. "Which one?" yelled the mate. "Both of them! This is more than just another Nor'easter!"

The ferry *Ocean Beach* left the dock en route to Bay Shore in the teeth of gale force winds, winds growing in intensity minute by minute. It snapped around, suddenly, blowing from the northwest, driving the ferry east. "Let out more scope!" Captain Garrett ordered. "The anchors aren't holding." The winds blew a steady 120 knots, gusting higher. The tide, already at its autumnal high, rose 12 to 15 feet in the bay twisting the *Ocean Beach* sideways, anchors dragging, waves pummeling its sides.

MEANWHILE IN SALTAIRE…

In one account, Barbara Overton Christie recalled that day: "'Radio says a storm's coming up,' a local man told Mother and I. 'Better batten down tight.' Sure enough, right after lunch the rains came. The lights suddenly went out, the radio dead. I opened the front door to check on the ocean just as a huge wave crashed over the dunes and swept in under our cottage. A larger wave followed, roaring past. 'We'd better get to Town Hall,' Mother shouted over the din. 'We don't want to get marooned.' Mother stuffed jewelry and some cash in her purse along with her favorite scissors, and a piece of jade a friend had given her for good luck. We started for the front door.

"A wall of water slammed over the dunes demolishing the boardwalk. We turned and rushed out the back door as a 25-foot high wave slammed into the cottage, sweeping us along with it, stumbling, water up to our knees. The cottage behind ours exploded into pieces. 'We need to get inside,' Mother cried. 'Anywhere!' We struggled toward a cottage still standing. The waves were breaking over the top of the houses and we were under them."

The ferry *Eladio* heaved wildly in the boat basin, its lines straining against the whipping winds and churning seas. The eye of the storm was approaching. Word was passed for everyone to retreat to the dock where the boat was waiting.

A 30-foot tidal wave breached the dunes. Houses were knocked off their foundations and floated away. Cottage ground against cottage. Boardwalk slats flew through the air.

Mrs. Marjorie Hopkins and her three children heard the homes breaking apart as they ran through the rising waters, a giant wave rolling after them. It kept coming. They stumbled aboard the *Eladio* and the ocean swept past.

Mary Frances Broadnax, a maid closing her employer's house for the season, never got the word to retreat to the dock. The house, only a block from the ocean, was suddenly smashed apart by breakers. She climbed up onto the roof through the hole where a chimney had once been just as the roof broke away and floated off. She jumped to a second roof with a stout chimney to which she clung for dear life.

Alice Trottier, her sister, Angeline Bazinet, and an elderly neighbor were up on the second floor playing cards when, without warning, the ocean was in the room with them, the house gone from around them. Alice, struggling to stay afloat, grabbed Angeline, who could not swim, by an arm, wrapping the other around a telephone pole, hanging on desparately. Their neighbor was gone.

THE *ELADIO* FOLLOWING THE HURRICANE OF '38.
Courtesy of FrankMina
http://saltairian.com/pages/history/1938/pictures1.html

BACK ON THE BAY

Captain Garrett put the helm hard over trying to turn the ferry's bow into the wind, hoping the anchors might catch, but they kept bouncing along the bottom. The boat broached, driven by 10 to 12 foot waves directly toward the Point O'Woods dock.

SALTAIRE

The Robinsons, a man, his wife Nora, and their son Billy, reached the cottage the same time as Mrs. Overton and her daughter. "We beat against the locked door as the seas beat against us," Christie recalled. "The door crashed open, the windows blew in. The thunder of the waves, the roar of the wind was deafening. Water quickly swamped the first floor chasing us up a rickety ladder, through a trap door, into the pitch black attic, so low our heads bent against the roof beams. The water was still rising and high tide was hours away. We were trapped."

The *Sea Horse*, a converted battleship tender, was docked near the *Eladio* which was already dangerously overloaded. Some passengers were transferring to the *Sea Horse* when a door carried aloft by the winds crashed through the windshield. The passengers quickly positioned planks over the broken window as wreckage—furniture, walls, doors, tree trunks, debris of all kinds—sailed through the air, hurled against the boats. The water in the basin was chock-a-block full of rubble so thick the boats could not maneuver. No one could leave.

FIRE ISLAND COAST GUARD STATION

Someone called the Coast Guard who dispatched an icebreaker, *AB25*, but because of the adverse conditions it could not reach the stranded refugees and was forced to anchor 15 miles to the east.

BACK IN SALTAIRE

Mary the maid spotted a larger roof and jumped for it. The roof floated away, Mary clutching desperately to its chimney through the teeming, drenching rains. The roof crashed into a cottage still anchored to its foundation. Mary clambered off the roof, through an attic window into the house. She barricaded the window with furniture and started praying.

George Baldwin, affectionately known as "Cappy," crippled from the waist down, was a tough bird living alone in his houseboat. That afternoon he was tending his "continuation stew," a pot to which he regularly added the catch-of-the-day. The locals swore the stew would kill him, but it didn't. The hurricane didn't kill him either. A roof gable slammed into his houseboat. Cappy grabbed onto the roof and, like Mary, became another roof-rider. Because of the impairment of his legs, Cappy had developed enormous upper body strength. He clung to the slick roof for five tortuous hours.

Mrs. Overton's pocketbook, full of jewels, her favorite scissors, and that piece of jade dropped through the trap door into the swirling waters below. The water level was still rising. They were to be drowned like unwanted kittens in the dark void of that black, claustrophobic attic.

OAKLEYVILLE/POINT O'WOODS

The ferry *Ocean Beach* ran down on the Point O'Woods dock pushed along by the violent wind-driven waves and hurricane winds. The dock, some 10 feet wide supported by wooden pilings, jutted out into bay directly in the path of the unchecked ferry. Its anchors, bouncing off the bay bottom had little effect on the heaving vessel. It rammed broadside into the dock, heeling violently. The momentum of the *Ocean Beach* drove it through the dock, destroying it, pushing the vessel up onto a sand bar off Oakleyville, aground.

CHERRY GROVE

Other ferries were also in action. Captain William Ryan rescued about 30 people from Cherry Grove and ferried them to Sayville in a harrowing two-hour trip with a compass he could not read because of the violent action of the boat and a windshield through which he could not see because of heavy salt spray.

The *Edward*, the boat Captain Warner used to deliver produce to the beach, picked up castaways at Cherry Grove also. However, it developed engine trouble and was driven eastward into Long Cove where it barely weathered the storm. Housemovers were needed to refloat the *Edward* once the hurricane had passed.

Saltaire Again

Little Billy cried, 'Mommy … where's my kitten?' 'Shush,' his Mommy whispered. 'She'll be alright.' His mother sang to him, later confiding to me that when the final crash came, she would hold his head under water so that he might drown quickly rather than being killed by the tempest. I looked down through the trap door, past our hanging feet, 'The water's stopped rising!'

'"Where are we?' someone asked. We were looking at the Great South Bay. The house in which we had found shelter was no longer near the ocean. It had sailed, with us in it, all the way across the island and become impaled on a telephone pole that kept us from being tossed into the frenzied waters of the bay.

The Robinson and Overton families staggered outside. The tide was receding and the wind was abating. "We broke into a lopsided cottage. Waves swept over its porch, but it was safer than our previous dwelling. Three inches of wet sand covered the first floor, but on the second we found dry clothes. Some wayward oranges provided a welcome feast. We cried and laughed and sang in joyous relief. The stars were out."

The survivors, huddling aboard the *Sea Horse* and the *Eladio* cheered the arrival of *AB25* with its food and hot coffee. After a brief repast, they set out for Village Hall finding dry shelter on its second floor. Groups of men set out on rescue missions—if there was anyone to rescue.

THE *SEAHORSE*, A CONVERTED 'BATTLESHIP
TENDER' BELONGING TO A MIKE COFFFEE WHERE THE
REFUGEES WAITED OUT THE STORM
http://saltairian.com/pages/history/1938/pictures1.html

Mary kept vigil from her furniture-barricaded perch in the attic. Her prayers were answered that evening when she was rescued by one of the searchers, Mike Coffey.

Alice's sister was torn from her arms and swept away. Alice hung onto the telephone pole until the wind moderated. She climbed down and crawled into the relative safety of a small roofless building. Mike Coffey found her too, and, arm around her waist, forced them through a half mile of detritus filled water, back to the dock, where they both collapsed from exhaustion.

"At dawn the five of us [The Robinsons and the Overtons] left our latest quarters, waded through waist-high water across a new inlet carved by the sea, and stumbled into Town Hall where we were greeted by 70 other survivors provisioning there."

OAKLEYVILLE

The crew and passengers aboard the *Ocean Beach* rode out the storm fast aground on the sand bar. As the storm passed, the ebbing waters rushed out of the bay leaving the boat heeled so far over that the fire extinguishers self-activated. But everyone was safe.

SALTAIRE

Mrs. Overton's pocketbook, which had dropped into the water as she scrambled up into the attic that afternoon, was found floating in the Great South Bay. Sodden and misshapen, it was returned to her anonymously in the mail. Still inside were her driver's license, some coins, her favorite scissors and—that piece of good-luck jade.

KISMET

A school had recently been opened in Kismet. It sported a steeple with a bell that tolled mournfully as the hurricane swept it away. The school was never rebuilt.

THE AFTERMATH...

Six Fire Islanders were killed—all in Saltaire.

The day after the storm, Thursday, Sept. 22, was a perfect day. The sea's rage had tempered. The sun was warm, the water calm, and the weather remained glorious for the rest of September.

After a hurricane there is a holy silence, like God has taken a deep breath and held it. "Even the birds seemed disoriented," one man said. "They come out—what birds were left—but they seemed spooky. They were as still as could be. They didn't sing or anything." Another man remembered, "Everything was beautifully clean after that. The next day and the next few weeks you never saw the air so clean. At night you could see stars you never could see before."

That was over 80 years ago.

Since then have come hurricanes Carol, and Gloria, the Frankenstorm, and, of course, Sandy. Who can forget Sandy?

What will be next?

A special thanks to Jim O'Hare for his help in compiling this article.

CAMP SIEGFRIED LONG ISLAND'S NAZI SUMMER RETREAT

A FLOWER BED WITH A SWASTIKA DESIGN AT THE CAMP SIEGFRIED SOCIAL CLUB GARDEN.

The need to commemorate *any* year in remembrance of those killed in the Nazi concentration camps is both sad and necessary.

The National Socialists Party of Germany, aka the Nazi Party, never painted the words "Only Aryan Lives Matter" on the pavement in front of grandstands from which Hitler preached his sermons of hate. They wrote those words, in blood, in our history books.

Although only in existence for 25 years the Nazi Party was responsible for 17 million deaths, 6 million Jews and 11 million others [Roma (Gypsies), the handicapped, political prisoners, religious dissenters, homosexuals, and prisoners of war].

As far removed as we may feel today from the horrors of those days—not really all that long ago—we need only to look across the bay to see what was happening not so far away. Within sight of Fire Island is a town called Yaphank. In the late 1930s, this town was home to the infamous Camp Siegfried, a summer camp that was owned by the German American Bund and operated by the German American Settlement League (GASL), a camp that openly taught Nazi ideology to boys and girls.

This innocent hamlet was founded in 1739, by Captain Robert Robinson. In the mid 18th century John Homan built two mills inspiring the town's name, Millville. It was later changed to Yaphank from the native Indian word Yamphanke, meaning "bank of a river."

IRVING BERLIN ID
Courtesy of John J. Gallagher Longwood Central School District Department of Music and Fine Arts

Yaphank has a rich history. During World War I, it was home to a boot camp called Camp Upton, used for training troops prior to their embarkation overseas. It was while stationed at Camp Upton that Irving Berlin composed his Broadway revue "Yip , Yip, Yaphank" that included the songs, "Oh! How I Hate to Get Up in the Morning," and "God Bless America," a song Berlin threw out because it was "too sticky" [his words.]

Camp Upton also has ties to Fire Island. In the early 1920s, the Perkinson family, who owned much of what is now Cherry Grove, decided to subdivide their property. They sold more than 100 plots for about $250 each to friends and relatives, some of whom also purchased government surplus homes from Camp Upton. They floated those homes across the bay to Fire Island, establishing the first large-scale settlement on the island [Point O' Woods also makes this claim].

In 1946, the government converted Camp Upton to the Brookhaven National Laboratory specializing in nuclear research, bioscience and nanoscience. The campus includes the Relativistic Heavy Ion Collider and National Synchrotron Light Source II. The lab has earned seven Nobel Prizes.

That was then, and time marches on—not always for the better. It was in Yaphank that Camp Siegfried opened in 1935. The property was owned by the German-American Bund and operated by the German-American Settlement League (GASL).

At its entrance both Nazi and Hitler Youth Flags flew alongside the American flag. It featured a social hall, a lake for swimming, a ball field, and a large white stage. The camp was opened expressly for the purpose of indoctrinating 150 to 300 boys and girls aged 8 to 18 in Nazi ideology. The children wore military uniforms and carried the banners of the Hitler Youth movement.

The Town of Brookhaven, in conjunction, approved an application for a nearby planned community called German Gardens.

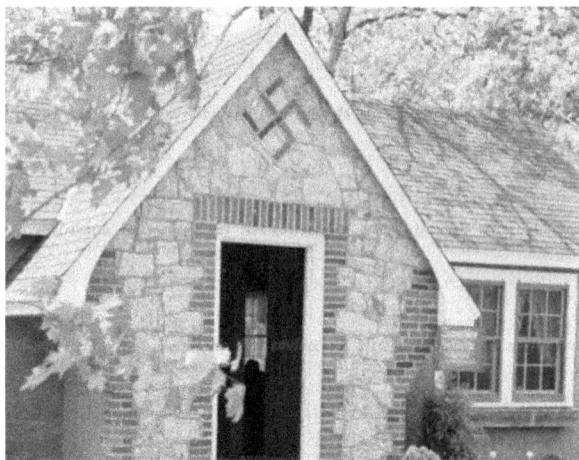

A "QUAINT" CAMP SIEGFRIED COTTAGE WITH A SWASTIKA INLAID IN THE MASONRY.

German Gardens had streets named after Adolf Hitler, Joseph Goebbels, and Hermann Goring, a community of 40 acres of small, well-kept bungalows. One home had the swastika inlaid in its roof shingles. A flower bed with a swastika design stood at the foot of the social club's flagpole.

Despite Nazi aversion to free market capitalism (it could not be trusted to put national interests first), the Bund ballyhooed their community and their camp with fervor.

German-Americans would catch the 8 a.m. LIRR "Camp Siegfried Special" to Yaphank and would march from the train station to the camp singing German songs. Some wore German folk costumes, some Nazi Brown Shirts, others the Black Shirts of Italian Fascists.

It was a family affair with a German folk-festival-flair complete with oom-pah-pah bands.

While some of the leaders and parents were zealous Nazis most were loyal to both America and Germany. At one point, August 1938, more than 40,000 people attended the annual German Day festivities at the camp.

SUCH COSTUMES LOOK OUT OF PLACE ON THE SLEEPY LONG ISLAND OF YAPHANK.

The children would compete in athletic competitions, swimming, hunting, and shooting. At night they would sit around bonfires singing the "Horst Wessel Song" and "Deutschland Uber Alles." To establish discipline the staff would occasionally waken the campers and take them on midnight marches through the woods.

The Bund was led by German-born Fritz Kuhn, who moved to the U.S. and became a naturalized citizen in 1934. Kuhn told the House Un-American Activities Committee that to join the Bund one had to be "Aryan," i.e. "a member of the white race." He claimed Bund membership of 20,000 with four or five times that many sympathizers. In a court case in 1938, one witness saluted the American flag with the Nazi salute. When asked if that was the American salute he replied, "It will be."

Kuhn was also the organizer of the infamous rally at Madison Square Garden where violence broke out in the street outside between Bund storm troopers and thousands of mostly Jewish protesters. One Jewish protester managed to reach the stage where Kuhn was mocking President Franklin D. "Rosenfeld." The protester had to be rescued by the NYC police after being stripped and beaten.

Later, Kuhn was found guilty of embezzlement and tax evasion and sentenced to prison. While in Sing-Sing he was stripped of his citizenship and, after the war, deported to Germany. In a comic Mel Brooks twist of fate, he was imprisoned for being a Nazi in the now Nazi-free Germany. He died in 1951 "a poor and obscure chemist, unheralded and unsung." [NY Times]

In 1940, the GASL took control of the camp announcing it would be non-political, but when Germany declared war the U.S. government seized the camp and shut it down forever.

The property called German Gardens still remained with GASL meaning that any sales had to be approved by the league. All owners had to be primarily of "German extraction." In 2006, this covenant caused problems when a couple tried to sell their property but could not because of its restrictions. New York State ruled that the clause violated the Fair Housing Act, and in 2017, the GASL was forced to change its by-laws and pay damages.

The names of the streets in German Gardens have all been changed. Adolf Hitler Street is now Park Street, Goering is now Oak, and Goebbels is Northside Avenue.

Most remembrances of its Nazi past have been erased but the clubhouse still stands, continuing to display both American and German flags.

But...

Time marches on dragging some of the vestiges of yesterday's hate along with it. Need we heed yesterday's deeds?

Stop for a moment. Dwell on those who died in death camps like Auschwitz, like Sobibor, like Treblinka. Millions of words have been written about the millions killed in those camps, but what has already been written is still millions of words short of what needs to be heard.

Photos courtesy of Municipal Records, City of New York
K. Cobb

ROBERT MOSES – A VISIONARY STRICKEN WITH MYOPIA

It is not hard to understand why Fire Islanders with knowledge of the island's history would dislike Robert Moses. He did, after all, try to jam a four-lane highway down the center of their island in spite of their vehement opposition.

ROBERT MOSES
Public domain

As ill-conceived as that notion was it is not representative of the visionary Robert Moses. He foresaw America's love affair with the automobile and its effect on city planning. He saw the automobile as a force not to be denied but as a force bound to revolutionize the landscape.

The future belonged to the automobile. His city planning reflected this single-minded, car-culture obsession for which he was later widely condemned. His critics assert that he cared more about cars than he did about people.

There is little question that Moses was arrogant. This arrogance transformed the young idealist into an old man obsessed with the acquisition and application of power, an obsession with getting things done, whatever the methods, whatever the costs. It, coupled with his idealism, enabled him to transform the New York environs as has no man before, or since, earning him the label "Master Builder."

The accomplishments of the man are so extensive that even the experts cannot quantify exactly how much he got done. He was responsible for the building of thirteen bridges, among them are the Bronx-Whitestone, the Throgs Neck, the Henry Hudson, the Triborough (now officially the Robert F. Kennedy Memorial Bridge), and the Verrazano–Narrows Bridge (his masterpiece).

VERRAZANO BRIDGE
Shawn Hoke CC BY-NC-ND 2.0

One of his major coups came when Mayor Fiorello La Guardia asked Moses to unify the City Parks Department. Moses drafted legislation creating the head of the department with himself as its multiyear commissioner. As such he was largely immune to pressure from mayors and/or governors.

While both New York City and New York State were continually broke, Moses' Triborough Bridge and

Tunnel Authority was awash in tens of millions of dollars generated by bridge, tunnel and road tolls which burgeoned as automobile use skyrocketed. Consequently, Moses was able to raise hundreds of millions dollars more by selling bonds enabling him to fund even more public construction projects.

But Moses did not pay off the bonds. Instead he built even more toll generating projects, a cycle that fed on itself, generating even more money. This scheme enabled Moses to proceed with his numerous plans with little outside interference. Genius!

Here is a list of Moses' accomplishments:
- The 1964 World's Fair.
- Jones Beach, which opened in 1930, was an overwhelming popular success. Thousands of visitors arrived on opening day and continue using the beach to this day.
- Grand Central, Southern State, Northern State, Interborough, Laurelton, Gowanus and Henry Hudson Parkways—416 miles of green, rolling parkways in all. Long Island's Meadowbrook Parkway was the first fully divided limited access highway in the world.
- The Brooklyn-Queens Expressway, Staten Island Expressway, the Cross-Bronx Expressway.
- Developed Stuyvesant Town, Washington Square Village, and Morningside Heights Chatham Towers creating 150,000 housing units.
- West Side Highway.
- FDR Drive.

- The United Nations complex including the Secretariat and General Assembly, buildings that straddle the FDR Drive.
- Lincoln Center for the Performing Arts.
- Shea Stadium.
- The 79th Street Boat Basin.
- The Jones Beach Marine Theater built for Guy Lombardo.
- In 1936 alone, he built 11 award winning swimming pools.
- 658 playgrounds.
- 300 basketball courts.
- He is responsible for increasing the total of number of acres of state park land from 9700 in 1928 to 2,567,256 in 1968.
- Two hydroelectric dams at Niagara Falls.
- In addition he also built schools, parks, piers, libraries, sewers, tunnels, beaches, zoos, civic centers, exhibition halls and golf courses.

1964 WORLD'S FAIR

At one point, Moses held twelve titles simultaneously, even though was never elected to any public office. In the 44 years that he was actively building, Moses constructed public works costing approximately 200 billion dollars in 2021 monies. At one point he had 80,000 people working for him. For years no public improvement was built without Moses express permission as to its design and location.

He worked 15 hours a day, sometimes more, without ever missing a good swim for exercise. He would leave envelopes of work orders he had done the previous night for his assistants to pick up and deliver to the appropriate agencies for completion the following day. The work was seldom completed on time.

And he was not in it for the money. As Park Commissioner his salary was a mere $13,600 dollars a year. As commissioner he consolidated the work of five borough park commissioners whose salaries totaled $62,000 dollars a year.

But he did take good care of himself. He had a staff of chauffeurs on call 24 hours a day to transport him to any one of his numerous offices throughout the city, many with personal chefs. Ironically, he never learned to drive. He never learned to drive but he never gave up on his belief in the automobile.

Eventually, his visionary beliefs were stricken with myopia. He failed to see the problems the proliferation of cars would cause, the twin problems of traffic jams, and pollution which would finally prove to be his demise. Even though he played no part in the wildly unpopular move of the Brooklyn Dodgers baseball team to L.A. in 1957, he got blamed for it anyway.

His arrogance was displayed when he would periodically offer his resignation believing himself to be indispensible. He was right—until 1962 when he offered it to then Governor Rockefeller who promptly accepted his resignation. Moses was on his way out.

In 1968, the Triborough Bridge and Tunnel Authority was merged into the new Metropolitan Transportation Authority. Moses was offered a job as consultant, but he refused, and retired to a small beach house in Gilgo, right across the inlet from Fire Island.

Robert Moses remained in office through five mayors, six Governors, and Seven Presidents from Coolidge thru Johnson.

He died on July 30, 1981 at the age of 92 of heart failure. Though of Jewish heritage, he had converted to Episcopalian and is interred in a crypt in Woodlawn Cemetery in the Bronx.

PROTECTING A RIBBON OF SAND

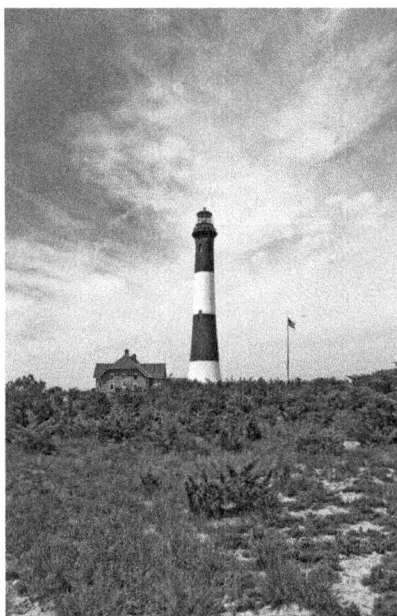

FIRE ISLAND LIGHTHOUSE
Erik Anestad licensed under CC BY 2.0

As part of the celebration of Fire Island National Seashore's 50th Anniversary, two sisters who grew up in Dunewood, Cathy and Susan Barbash, curated an exhibition at the Fresnel Lens building at the Fire Island Lighthouse: "Protecting a Ribbon of Sand: The Creation of Fire Island National Seashore."

The exhibit contained the chronology of events that led up to how Fire Island ultimately became incorporated into the National Park Service, focusing on the decades-long fight with Robert Moses over his plans for a four-lane highway down the center of Fire Island. It was Moses' plan and the local residents' fight to prevent it that led to the successful formation of, the Fire Island National Seashore (FINS).

The exhibit was dedicated in memory of Maurice Barbash, their father, who as President of the Citizen's Committee for a Fire Island National Seashore was instrumental in its creation as he lobbied both on Long Island and in Washington D.C. It's an exciting story, full of defeats and victories, acted out by a cast of characters straight out of central casting.

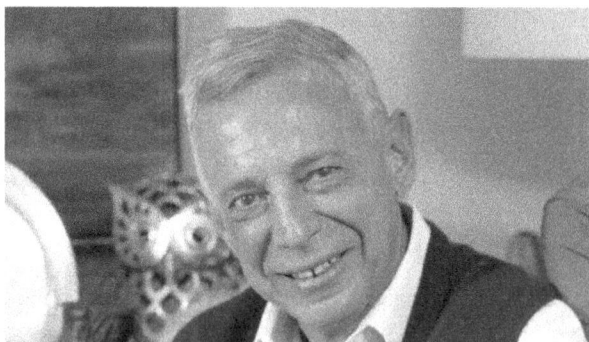

MURRAY BARBASH
Courtesy of Susan Barbash

THE FIGHT BEGINS

In 1924, Robert Moses proposed a road stretching from the Rockaways to Montauk. His proposal took on extra import when he was named Long Island State Park Commission Chairman and the Commission started developing construction plans for the road.

After several hurricanes devastated Fire Island (particularly the Long Island Express – hurricane of '38),

Moses pushed again for the road, under the guise of "stabilizing" the island, but WWII intervened.

In 1957, Congressman Wainwright of East Hampton introduced several bills to create a national seashore, but they died because of lack of local support. In 1953 Cape Hatteras was designated the first National Seashore, followed by Fire Island in 1964 and Cape Cod in 1966, but that was still off in the future.

Rachel Carson published "Silent Spring," in 1962 awakening environmental awareness. The pot was bubbling.

After the Ash Wednesday storm in March of 1962, Moses resuscitated his plans, again emphasizing halting beach erosion. He had the support of Suffolk County Executive H. Lee Dennison as well as Long Island's most popular newspaper, *Newsday*. In June of '62, the road proposal was actually approved by the Temporary State Commission on the Protection and Preservation of the Atlantic Shore Front.

However U.S. Secretary of the Interior Stewart Udall offered a master plan to preserve the East Coast shores. He toured Fire Island by helicopter, and subsequently wrote a letter of support of the seashore. That same month the *New York Times* published an editorial supporting declaration of Fire Island as a national seashore.

THEN THE FUN BEGAN

Sensing a growing opposition to Moses' road, the aforementioned Temporary State Commission scheduled a July meeting at Jones Beach. A thousand people were turned away from what quickly developed into a raucous assembly.

One woman carrying a sign reading, "He thinks he's God, but he's only Moses," was quickly hustled away. Numerous opponents to the road were prevented from speaking. Segments of the media were locked out. CBS correspondent Charles Collingwood compared Moses to Hitler. As Moses stormed out, he was asked about the opposition of the island's residents. He replied that there are no Fire Island residents, only summer visitors.

The New York Times, The New Yorker Magazine, and even *Sports Illustrated*, covered the chaotic meeting much to Moses' chagrin, but in spite of all the opposition, not one of the 15 commission members wavered in their support for Moses' road.

IRVING LIKE
Courtesy of Susan Barbash

THE BATTLE WAXES

Unwilling to be trampled by Moses' heavy-handed tactics, the citizens of Fire Island rose up. Maurice Barbash and Irving Like founded the Citizens Committed for a Fire Island National Seashore, announcing its support for a national seashore designation and its opposition to the road.

Like a giant dusting off flies, the State Commission adopted plans for the highway, once again citing stabilization of the beach. Adding insult to injury, the Suffolk County Planning Commission endorsed Moses' plan, as did the Suffolk County Board of Supervisors.

Representative Otis Pike (D – NY), stated he would vote in favor of the road, and *Newsday* also editorialized in favor of Moses.

But Barbash and Like continued swaying public opinion in their favor. They addressed numerous governmental, scientific, and conservation groups outlining their arguments for the need for the Fire Island National Seashore (FINS).

OCEAN PARKWAY
Dougtone CC BY-SA 2.0 Copy

The media discovered that Moses' Ocean Parkway required a constant supply of beach sand to keep the road intact. The beach did not need to be stabilized by the road. The road needed the beach sand to stabilize it. Pike, realizing that his position was losing favor among his constituents, moderated his position. He would oppose the road, but was still not in favor of FINS.

THE END IS NEAR

In the much-fabled climactic encounter, Nelson Rockefeller, governor of New York, and Robert Moses met to discuss Laurence Rockefeller's (the governor's brother and an ardent conservationist) interference with Moses' agenda. The two titans clashed, and Moses threatened to resign, a common tactic of his that had never before failed. Rockefeller accepted his resignation, and Moses was, for the most part, through.

Months went by. Udall was committed to FINS, while Pike was telling the Suffolk County Board of Supervisors that the seashore was a dead issue. Little by little however, public support for the idea grew. *Newsday* moderated its position, first agreeing that the best solution was for a section of Fire Island to be "genuinely wild," and then agreeing that since Moses' road appeared to be dead, it was in favor of FINS.

In April of '63 Citizens Committee Chair Maurice Barbash led a delegation to meet with Secretary Udall, and shortly thereafter the *New York Times* and *Newsday* both urged rapid passage of FINS legislation.

With the tide rushing in to drown him, Pike finally reversed his position, expressing his support. This was a crucial change because Congress was controlled by the Democrats at that time. Pike was a Democrat, and a Democrat was needed to introduce the bill.

Finally on Sept. 11, 1964, President Johnson signed Public Bill 88-587, establishing the Fire Island National Seashore.

The story of Fire Island National Seashore has been told well in many local histories available today, however the Barbash sisters made it fresh and accessible in a concise visual format, thanks to fastidious research and the first hand experience of growing up with a family active in the cause. Well done Cathy and Susan Barbash!

IRVING LIKE:
AN INTERVIEW WITH THE LAST SURVIVING MEMBER OF THE CITIZEN'S COMMITTEE FOR THE FIRE ISLAND NATIONAL SEASHORE

IRVING LIKE
Courtesy of Ernie Fazio info@limba.net

Irving Like is a long time resident of Dunewood and one of the primary movers and shakers in defeating Robert Moses' plan for a four-lane highway down the center of

Fire Island from the Robert Moses causeway to Smith Point, Mastic Beach. Irving, as he prefers to be called, is in his early nineties and still going strong, strong enough to be actively involved with plans to get Fire Island Seashore designated as a World Heritage Site. No small dreams for this man.

Besides defeating Moses by implementing the creation of the Fire Island National Seashore, the many other projects in which Irving has been involved include legislation requiring medical coverage for Viet Nam veterans exposed to Agent Orange and defeating the Shoreham Nuclear power plant. He also defeated CON ED's Storm King Mountain power plant. He is the author of the Conservation Bill of Rights, which has been incorporated as Article 14 of the NY State Constitution. He also authored the Nature Preservation clause of the Suffolk County Charter.

Among his legal clients have been; Great South Bay Association; Friends of the Fire Island National Seashore; Fire Island Association; Village of Saltaire; NY Coastal Partnership; Appalachian Mountain Club, and many, many others A complete list of all of Irving's accomplishments would take up more space than this column is allowed. He is a Fire Island treasure and we all are indebted to him for everything he has done.

***

FIN: Good afternoon, Mr. Like.

LIKE: Good afternoon. Please call me Irving.

FIN: Where did you grow up, Irving?

LIKE: I was born in Brooklyn, but went to James Monroe high school in the Bronx. My high school days only lasted three years because of the war. That's WW 2. I served in the Signal Corps where they taught us Russian. I believe the plan was for us to bomb Japan from the Russian peninsula, Kamchatka, but the war ended first.

We were also schooled in military intelligence. (Irving chuckles.) We were supposed to learn to use foreign language maps, making our way back to Camp Richie—it's called Camp David now. It was night and we got lost. Luckily, we found a farmhouse with a light on. The farmer gave us directions or we would never have successfully completed the exercise.

FIN: Where did you get your law degree?

LIKE: After the war, I attended Columbia Law School where I got my degree.

FIN: When did you get involved with Fire Island?

LIKE: I bought a cottage in Dunewood back in the 1950s. My sister, Lillian, married Murray Barbash who had purchased a large section of Fire Island, subdivided it, and started building homes on those plots. He named the area Dunewood, and I've maintained a cottage there ever since.

FIN: What was your role implementing the Fire Island National Seashore?

LIKE: About 1962 Robert Moses came up with the idea of building a four-lane road down the center of Fire Island. Those of us who lived on the island were against this idea from the very start. It would have ruined the ecology and beauty the island. Something had to be done, but we did not know how to stop such a powerful man. Don't forget that Moses was responsible for projects like Jones Beach. They even named the bridge from Bay Shore to Fire Island after him.

FIN: So what did you do?

LIKE: Well, when I learned about the National Seashores at Cape Cod and Cape Hatteras, I came up with the idea of creating a National Seashore for Fire Island. We formed the Citizens Committee for the Fire Island National Seashore and cobbled together a draft for the idea. At one point, even the Hamptons wanted to be included within the seashore boundaries, but that idea was quickly scrapped.

Next was to sell the idea to the public, both those on the island and the mainland. It took two years for opinion to shift in favor of the seashore mainly because the newspapers finally came around to our way of thinking. They were led by Alicia Patterson, who was the owner and editor of *Newsday* at the time. Otis Pike, who was a Democratic congressman back then, became the lead proponent of the bill. Priscilla Roe of The Patchogue League of Women Voters and Carly Larson were two spark plugs on the mainland who pushed hard for the bill. In fact, Roe would call Brookhaven Supervisor Charles Dominy at 7 am each morning, kind of poking at him, but they actually developed a friendship, and that helped too. The bill finally got it adopted by Congress in 1964.

(Irving laughs.) The final nail in the coffin for Moses' highway idea came when we discovered that his main argument in favor of the road was that the road would anchor the dunes in place when in fact he was spending money to protect the roads along Ocean Parkway from erosion.

FIN: Have you ever considering retiring?

LIKE: (Chuckles.) No. There is too much going on. I am involved in the Shore Erosion Project, replacing the dunes lost to Sandy and other storms while protecting the rights of the property owners affected by moving back the dunes – the compensation and easement issues, but my main concern these days is getting the Fire Island National Seashore designated as a World Heritage Site.

Jerry Stoddard, who retired as president of the Fire Island Association not long ago, and I are actively involved in getting the Fire Island Seashore designated as a World Heritage Site.

Here's a news scoop for you. We have enlisted the help of Dr. John Tanacredi, head of Environmental Sciences at Malloy College, and Dr. Ron Abrams, another renowned PhD Ecologist. Tanacredi was involved in getting Easter Island designated as a World Heritage Site and Abrams has experience with South Africa World Heritage Site activity. Stony Brook University has also joined us.

A couple of others who are with us that I should mention are Ronald Lee of the National Park Service, and Charles Callison, Executive Director of the National Audubon Society. Callison told me, "Some losing causes are worth fighting for." I have no plan of losing, however.

The Fire Island Seashore is a natural symbol of peace. The only other World Heritage Site in New York is the Statue of Liberty, a worldwide symbol of peace. A World Heritage Site designation would be a gesture of peace, and with the Pope's latest encyclical about climate change anything seems possible. Any acknowledgement from the Pope would go a long way in helping our cause.

(Irving laughs again.) Stoddard and I joke that we are probably involved in a project that will not be resolved until we are long gone.

FIN: What do you consider the odds of getting the Fire Island Seashore designated as a World Heritage Site?

LIKE: (Sits up straight.) ONE HUNDRED PERCENT!

FIN: That's pretty optimistic.

LIKE: Well, keep in mind what Margaret Mead said, and I paraphrase here, "Never doubt that a small group of committed citizens can change the world. It's the only thing that ever has."

FIN: Considering all your accomplishments, of what are you most proud?

LIKE: (Hesitates for several moments.) I'm most proud of my kids. I have a daughter, Sharon, a single mom—a full time job in itself—who is also supervising counsel for the Federal Finance Agency. My son, Robert, is a doctor and a professor at Rutgers Medical School. He was selected as the Master Teacher of the Year. And, of course, I've been married to my wife, Margalit, for 66 years. (Chuckles) I decide if the U.S. should go to war or not. She decides everything else.

GENERAL GEORGE C. MARSHALL
AND FIRE ISLAND

General George C. Marshall (December 31, 1880 – October 16, 1959) recipient of the 1953 Nobel Peace Prize and author of the internationally acclaimed and hugely successful Marshall Plan was a resident of Ocean Beach, Fire Island for over twenty years, from the summer of 1930 until 1951.

GEORGE C. MARSHALL, FRONT ROW, THIRD FROM THE LEFT, JUNE 5, 1947. ALSO PRESENT ARE, FRONT ROW, FAR LEFT: J. ROBERT OPPENHEIMER; THIRD FROM THE RIGHT, GENERAL OMAR BRADLEY; AND SEATED TO THE GENERAL'S LEFT, T. S. ELIOT. THESE MEN WERE ALL GRANTED HONORARY DEGREES THIS DAY.
Public Domain

The house on Bayberry where he stayed was originally purchased by his second wife, Katherine Tupper

Brown in 1928. His first visit was in 1930 at the invitation of Katherine so that he could meet her three children, Allen, Clifton, and Molly. While the younger two children had no problem with the invitation, Allen, then twelve, told his mother, "I don't know about that, we are happy enough as we are." By the next morning he had changed his mind and sent Marshall a letter in which he wrote, "I hope you will come to Fire Island. Don't be nervous, it is OK with me." He signed it, "A friend in need is a friend indeed. Allen Brown. The visit went well and Marshall and Katherine were married that October

Marshall visited Katherine and the children as often as possible, but, given the demands of his duties, the visits were sporadic and usually brief. In a letter to General John J. Pershing in 1935 he wrote: "Molly [his step-daughter] had landed from her ten month trip around the world, on June 5th, and had opened the cottage. Allen came up from the University of Virginia at the same time. He 'life guards' at thirty bucks a week. Has made ten rescues in the heavy surf."

In an unhappy twist of fate, Allen Tupper Brown was shot and killed by a sniper on May 29, 1944. He was posthumously awarded the Bronze Star.

After the hurricane of 1938, on September 26 in another letter to General Pershing, Marshall wrote of the harrowing experiences his wife experienced during that hurricane. "I returned to Washington Wednesday afternoon, and Thursday morning learnt of the terrific hurricane in the Northeast. The Western Union people told me I could not hope to communicate with Bay Shore, L.I., the point from which one takes a boat for Fire Island, where Mrs. Marshall has her cottage, for at least 24 hours; and as nothing was known of what had occurred on Fire Island, I took a plane and flew up to see what had occurred. From the air, I saw the cottage had not been destroyed, though most of the houses in the vicinity had collapsed or been demolished. Many on the bay side of the island—which is about 600 yards wide—had floated out in the water. On the ocean side, the dunes had been broken through by heavy seas and most of the cottages in that vicinity were destroyed. I flew over to Mitchel Field and procured a small training plane, and succeeded in landing on the beach. I found Mrs. Marshall and Molly all right, but they had had a terrific night and escaped from the cottage in water up to their waists, and in a 50-90 mile an hour gale. My orderly was with them and he did his part nobly. The next morning they took stock and found that the cottage had not been harmed, though destruction elsewhere had been terrific, and quite a few lives were lost. The adjacent community of Saltaire was completely destroyed, except for 6 cottages. I remained on the island and got Mrs. Marshall over to the Long Island side. On Friday evening I took her and Molly in to New York, where they now are, apparently none the worse for their experience."

This is the same hurricane, sometimes called "The Long Island Express," that killed 600 people and caused over $4 billion dollars in damages.

Cameron Dunbar, a resident of Ocean Beach recalled his encounters with the General. "When I was about ten years old, General Marshall came to Ocean Beach in an Army amphibian plane to visit [Katherine]. When the plane came in near the beach on the bay side, the tide was too low, and, therefore, they couldn't get close enough to the shore to disembark. I saw them, rowed out to the plane, and then backed the rowboat against it. General Marshall hopped on, and I rowed him to shore. He gave me a tip. General Marshall only came to visit three or four times each summer, but after that day he would always circle Ocean Beach each time he came to visit and I would come from wherever I was to meet him in the rowboat."

In 1939 President Franklin D. Roosevelt promoted Marshall to Army Chief of Staff. In just three years in that capacity, he transformed a rag-tag, ill-equipped Army of less than 200,000 men into a formidable fighting force of over 8 million soldiers. This feat was instrumental in the defeat of the Axis forces in WWII. He was promoted to a four-star general the same day Hitler invaded Poland, the act that triggered the war.

The Army built a secret passage with a trap door in the house in which Marshall spent his time on Fire Island just in case either the Germans or Japanese came for him. Yet as much as he enjoyed his retreats to the island they eventually came to exasperate him. With the war fully engaged, in a letter dated May 14, 1941 he wrote: "I had good luck on the weather this trip, but a little bad luck otherwise. We were simply pestered to death by people coming in to talk over 'the situation.' A perfect stranger got into the house Saturday night and stayed for 2 hours. We went down town for dinner Saturday and I practically did not get to eat, as someone seemed always standing beside the table—being very pleasant and gracious but making it pretty difficult to get any relaxation. Fire Island has always been free of this sort of thing, so I was disappointed."

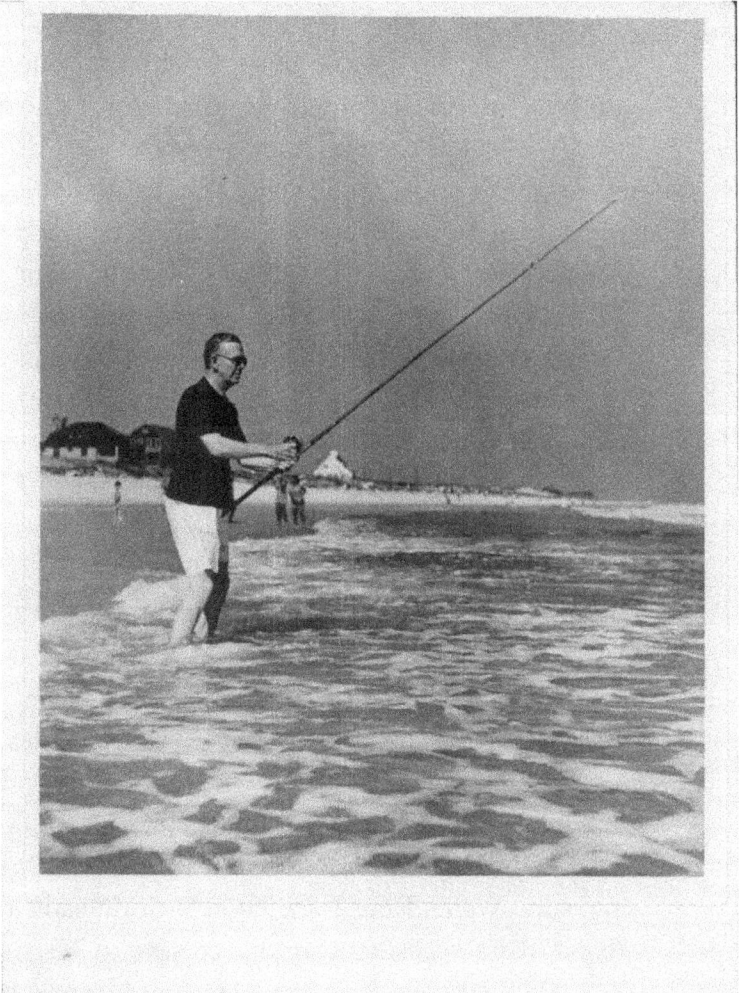

GENERAL GEORGE C. MARSHALL SURF-
CASTING ON FI, SUMMER 1938
Courtesy of the George C. Marshall Foundation, Lexington, Virginia

Marshall, "almost six feet tall, ramrod-straight,
invariably proper, impeccably controlled, and determinedly
soft-spoken," had hoped to become the Supreme Allied
Commander in Europe, but President Franklin D. Roosevelt

would not part with him due to his superior planning and diplomatic skills. "I could not sleep nights, George," FDR told him, "if you were out of Washington." The Supreme Allied Commander title went to Dwight D. Eisenhower instead.

But he was by no means overlooked for his accomplishments. *Time* magazine named Marshall their "Man of the Year" in 1943 and British Prime Minister Winston Churchill praised him as the "organizer of the Allied victory." In 1944 he was made a five-star General, the first in history.

Wally Pickard, one of five generations of Pickards who have called Fire Island home for decades, became General Marshall's aide. He joined the Army Air Corps and had been sent to Hickham Field in Hawaii to await further orders. The Japanese attacked Pearl Harbor the following morning and Pickard was severely wounded.

Wally's mother, not having heard from her son for two days, became concerned and asked Marshall's wife, Katherine, to please see what she could discover. Katherine asked the General who took immediate action. Wally was shipped to Walter Reed Hospital in D.C. He had almost lost a hand, but a specialist was able to save it. Marshall, who Wally said was "a kind man but aloof," took a special interest in Wally and assigned him as his aide, serving in adjacent offices at the Pentagon. Ever the optimist, Wally credits his wounds with exposing him to that "great experience that few men would ever have, something I can be proud of," and, not incidentally, with saving his life. In a taped interview Wally ruminated: "Had I not been wounded in Pearl Harbor I would not have been fortunate enough to be talking to you. [Richard Hein, the interviewer] Could have been worse. I just know I'm lucky. And here I am talking to you. June 22nd, 2008, a beautiful day on Fire Island. Oh yeah, said it was going to rain. Sure doesn't look like rain."

It is rumored that Wally holds the record for the most consecutive summers on Fire Island. He was brought over by his parents before his first birthday and returned every year, including the war years, until his death at the age of 93.

With the war behind him, George Marshall resigned his commission in 1945 to become President Truman's special diplomatic envoy and in 1947 he accepted appointment as Secretary of State. In this capacity he drew up plans for aiding Europe's recovery from WWII.

PRESIDENT HARRY TRUMAN AND SECRETARY OF STATE GEORGE MARSAHLL 1948
Public Domain

Millions had died in the war. European industries had been all but destroyed; its infrastructure lay in ruins. Famine loomed. On June 5, 1947 at Harvard University's commencement, Marshall delivered a ten minute speech outlining the European Recovery Program. Many in government wanted to call this the Truman Plan but the President insisted that it be called the Marshall Plan. In 1947 *Time* magazine, once again, selected Marshall as their "Man of the Year."

Marshall retired in 1951. He and Katherine sold their home in Ocean Beach and moved to Dedona Manor in Leesburg, Virginia, about which he said "this is Home...a real home after 41 years of wandering." The house, now known as the Marshall House, is a National Historic Landmark and a museum.

In 1953 George C. Marshall won the Nobel Peace Prize for the Marshall Plan. He is the only military officer to ever win this prize and about which he said in his Nobel acceptance speech, "There has been considerable comment over the awarding of the Nobel Peace Prize to a soldier. I am afraid this does not seem as remarkable to me as it quite evidently appears to others. I know a great deal of the horrors and tragedies of war. Today, as chairman of the American Battle Monuments Commission, it is my duty to supervise the construction and maintenance of military cemeteries in many countries overseas, particularly in Western Europe. The cost of war in human lives is constantly spread before me, written neatly in many ledgers whose columns are gravestones. I am deeply moved to find some means or method of avoiding another calamity of war. Almost daily I hear from the wives, or mothers, or

172

families of the fallen. The tragedy of the aftermath is almost constantly before me."

George C. Marshall died in 1959 at the age of 78, and is interred at Arlington National Cemetery.

We can be proud that a man of such accomplishments chose to wrest from his tumultuous life whatever leisure he could here on the sands of Fire Island.

This article was originally prepared to commemorate the 70th Anniversary of General George Marshall's famous speech delivered at Harvard University on June 5, 1947. This speech is often credited to opening the gateway to the program known as The Marshall Plan for which Marshall won the Nobel Peace Prize.

THE FIRE ISLAND SUMMER CLUB –
A DIFFERENT KIND OF
COMMUNITY

FIRE ISLAND SUMMER CLUB is one of the lesser known of the 16 individual and distinct communities on Fire Island. It is located between Corneille Estates, a mere two-block walk from the infamous metropolis of Ocean Beach on the east, and the Fire Island National Seashore (FINS) on the west.

The Summer Club was incorporated in 1946, founded by members of the New York Athletic Club who envisioned a non-profit, private-membership, family community along the lines of Point O' Woods. It was originally called The Fire Island Beach Club, and was organized to never be over-populated or commercialized, with all members bound by the rules and bylaws of the club.

The community was initially divided into 79 lots with additional land reserved for a clubhouse and two tennis courts. The original 50 members were required to put up an initiation fee of $150 and pay annual dues of $50 a year. If they wanted to participate in the land development project they were required to ante up an additional $150.

In the summer of 1947, it was determined that the cost of an individual lot would be $1,500 with a limit of two lots per member. Lots were leased for 99 years and development was slow with only six homes completed by the end of 1947, two more in 1950, with an expectation of

10 more by the end of that year. Many of the lots remained vacant until the 1970s. Today there are 44 individual single-family homes, with rights to both ocean and bay beaches, bayside mooring for their boats and membership in their clubhouse.

The sale of 44 plots to 27 of the original members in the fall of 1946, along with option rights and additional assessments, provided the funds necessary to purchase the clubhouse, along with equipment, cement walkways and other improvements.

The Remarkable History of the Summer Beach Clubhouse

FIRE ISLAND SUMMER CLUB BOUND: FLOATING THE DECOMMISSIONED COAST GUARD STATION ON THE GREAT SOUTH BAY.
Public Domain

The clubhouse was originally one of seven United States Life Saving Stations (USLSS) located about five miles apart along the length of Fire Island. It is said that an early club member, one Mr. Murphy, a Navy veteran, was instrumental in the purchase of the Blue Point station, which turned out to have a remarkable history all its own.

Throughout the early maritime history of America there were untold numbers of shipwrecks along the East Coast resulting in the loss of hundreds of lives and uncounted dollars in property damage.

In order to aid these stricken vessels, their crews and passengers, several small buildings, equipped with the most basic equipment and supplies, were constructed. They were unmanned, but serviced by a volunteer force usually made up of baymen and farmers. As traffic increased along the East Coast, the United States Life Saving Service (USLSS) was established in 1878, with stations located from Maine to North Carolina, and then on to Florida.

Eventually these unmanned rescue shacks grew in size until by the turn of the century they housed a crew and often consisted of several buildings with the main structure sporting a lookout tower on its roof.

FIRE ISLAND LIFE SAVING STATION.

FIRE ISLAND LIFE SAVING STATION WITH
LIGHTHOUSE IN BACKGROUND C. 1848
Courtesy of Suffolk County Historical Society Library Archives

The seven USLSS located on Fire Island were the Fire Island Station, Point O' Woods, Lone Hill (FI Pines), Blue Point (Water Island), Bellport, Smith Point and Forge River (Moriches Inlet).

It was the Blue Point Coast Guard Station, built in 1913, that was purchased as the Summer Beach Club clubhouse and is the only one left in its original configuration—less modern improvements. Another incorporated into Flynn's Hotel in Ocean Bay Park.

These stations are responsible for aiding 721 vessels and saving 7,086 lives with the Blue Point Station responsible for approximately 80 of those rescues according to the Summer Club website (summerclubfi.com).

Among the more harrowing stories of shipwrecks on Fire Island and one in which the Blue Point Station was directly involved, was that of the loss of both the *Louis V. Place* and *John B. Manning*, which took place over three days in February 1895. The story tells of frozen crew-members hanging in the rigging and the heroic attempts to save them. Seven men were lost, including the captain, and only one survived. You can read the complete story here and also at greaterpatchoguehistoricalsociety.com

The Blue Point Station is also famous for the two gold lifesaving medals awarded by the U.S. Coast Guard to surfmen Frank B. Raynor and Albert Latham for their heroism in saving lives after the wreck of the schooner *Benjamin C. Cromwell* in February of 1904. These heroic men actually entered the freezing ocean in the middle of the winter and pulled survivors ashore.

The USLSS stations were transferred to Coast Guard operations in 1915, and continued to operate through WWII after which the stations were decommissioned and declared government surplus. The Summer Beach Club purchased the Blue Point Station building for $3,500 dollars and floated it down the Great South Bay to its present location.

Food was served on weekends through the '50s, and on Saturday nights in the '60s the clubhouse held dances including hosting Woody Allen's jazz band.

WOODY ALLEN JAZZ BAND

From the '50s through the '70s a boat basin and dock occupied property to the west of the clubhouse. This property was deeded to the National Park Service and is now a permanent part of the Fire Island National Seashore.

Summer Club Condominiums – A Self-Managed Community

In the early 1990s, the name of the community was changed from the Fire Island Summer Club to Summer Club Condominiums. Today the bay front clubhouse hosts social events each season and features a full-workout fitness center and gaming tables.

Renovations to the clubhouse, including a new bar, are now a fait accompli. In addition, a new dock has been installed for use exclusively by the Summer Club residents—no ferries or water taxis land there. The budget for these improvements was $400,000.

What sets the Summer Club apart from other Fire Island communities is that it is organized as a self-governed condominium complex with strict rules run by a nine-member board of directors. The homes are owner occupied with limited allowance for group rentals. No new two-story construction is permitted to maintain open spaces and views. The Summer Club has its own security on its beaches. They also have an electric golf cart to aid in transporting residents to and from the Ocean Beach ferry dock. This strong self-management has allowed the Summer Club to accumulate a substantial reserve fund, and keep maintenance low.

The Fire Island Summer Club is another pearl in the necklace of communities that make up Fire Island.

WOLCOTT GIBBS – FIRE ISLAND MELLOWS A CURMUDGEON

"Backward ran sentences until reeled the mind," reads Wolcott Gibbs' parody of *Time* magazine, a piece still highly touted, so much so that it tends to obscure much of what else he wrote, and write he did. Gibbs concluded his lampoon, "Where it all will end, knows God!"

WOLCOTT GIBBS
Courtesy of Troy Seckerth

Wolcott Gibbs wrote for *The New Yorker* from 1927 until his death in 1958. He was an editor, a theatre critic, an author of short stories, a Broadway playwright, a humorist with a wicked wit, and he was a Fire Islander.

He was also a condescending curmudgeon, an unhappy boy who grew into a less happy man. He came from a family that once had bucks but then had none, a family that fought to protect its highbrow pedigree.

He was named after Oliver Wolcott, a signer of the Declaration of Independence, was also a direct descendent of Martin Van Buren, President of the United States, for chrissakes. But then his father had to go and die on him, him being only six, and his mother loses custody of her own children because she's a drunk, so he and his sister are raised by a bachelor uncle who never settled down, took them everywhere and nowhere.

If only he'd gone to college! He complained so often his friends threatened to raise enough money to send him to Yale for a weekend just to shut him up. No wonder Gibbs became known for his disdain for his fellow man, for his cheeky rudeness, for chrissakes. He once wrote, "I wonder if there is something the matter with me that I can't like anybody for long." He was never happy—never happy, that is, except on Fire Island.

He found Fire Island as a child, sailing over one day with some cousins and that was it. It was like falling in love with the perfect woman, not that *that* ever happened to him of course. He was married three times.

First time was a strike-out with a Miss Too-Young—neither of them ever spoke of it afterwards.

Second time he was already a dandy-drudge with damaged dreams. Three years of marriage hell until she threatened to jump out the 17th story window and he told her to go ahead and she did. Dead.

Third time's a charm it's said. Well, certainly not charmed for Gibbs. Maybe he and Elinor loved each other, but then again maybe not. They sure loved getting sloshed together and get sloshed they did.

His one true love, the novelist Nancy Hale, had to be a married woman, of course, with a son of her own, of course. The affair was brief (she broke it off, of course), but he continued to write love notes for years. "I am never going to be in love with anybody but you," he wrote, "and I suppose I might as well get used to the idea in spite of all the nervous breakdowns it gives me." He shared his love affair with Fire Island with her too. "I am a child of the sun, and in the summer I am happy, singing from morning till night, but when it gets cold I die."

She never responded, of course.

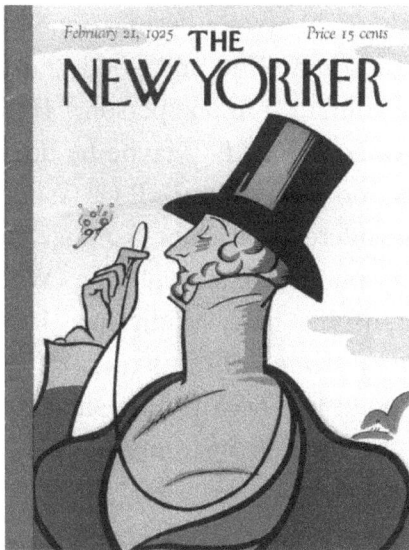

EUSTACE TILLEY GRACES THE COVER OF THE FIRST
ISSUE OF THE NEW YORKER MAGAZINE
Public Domain

He was a successful writer, wrote for *The New Yorker* for thirty years. In his role as a critic, he wrote the most succinct review of a play ever. The play was called "Wham!" and his critique was "Ouch!" Another oft quoted review was of William Saroyan's "The Beautiful People." Gibbs opened by describing "a set that might have been executed by Salvador Dali, needing, in fact, only a rubbery watch and a couple of lamb chops." But writing reviews, even for plays on Broadway, he shook his head, was no way for a serious writer to make a living.

Oh yeah, there was his Broadway play, "Season in the Sun." It was an accumulation of his stories written for *The New Yorker*, about, yep, you guessed it, Fire Island. Ran for 10 months. Not bad. Not "Guys and Dolls," mind you, but counting money is so boorish anyway.

Giants of his time heaped praise. E. B. White (*Charlotte's Web*) wrote, "professionally ambidextrous: a natural editor, a prolific and good and versatile writer—gifts rarely combined in one person." Harold Ross, founder of *The New Yorker* said, "Maybe he doesn't like anything, but he can do everything." P.G. Wodehouse (*My Man Jeeves*) considered *The New Yorker* "the dullest bloody thing ever published...except for Wolcott Gibbs." In admiration of his nasty witticisms James Thurber (*The Secret Life of Walter Mitty*) wrote, "When Wolcott Gibbs set out to do 'a job' on a profile subject, he brought out a fine array of surgical instruments, a rapier, and a pearl-handled blackjack."

Gibbs was good for a few hours at a party, not that he enjoyed parties—hated them—all that mixing with his inferiors, most of whom did not possess enough manners to leave him to his booze. He hated introductions obliging him to know people he would rather avoid. "Every man seems threatening to become my brother or better," he complained. Didn't anyone read Emily Post anymore, for chrissakes?

A couple of hours of free-flowing booze and he was liquefied. His friends would pour him into the backseat of a taxi for the black-out home. The only problem was putting all the disconnected memories back together again the next day. His insults, he remembered, were always the acme, never *ba-nal*. He left that to lesser men.

Fire Island was the only lady who ever made him happy—yes, happy. "I'm in love with the goddam beach!" he crowed. He loved the sun and the sand, cigarettes, and martinis. He would mix a shaker full, take it to the beach and bury it up to its neck in the sand. He'd lie in the sun, chain-smoking cigarettes, and drinking of course. He'd sunbathe all day, tanning his skin, and bleaching his hair. **Russell Maloney,** one of his drinking buddies, remarked that Gibbs looked like a "photographic negative" of himself, which, of course, he was. But at least the island made him happy—a curmudgeon mellowed by Fire Island.

He even started a local paper, *The Fire Islander,* where he tempered his sardonic edge with, dare it be said, almost sunny copy. He enlisted his comrades from *The New Yorker* in his new endeavor—got them to write pieces for his baby. Never paid them, of course, but he might take them out to lunch.

His paper was genuinely concerned about his island—ever so serious about it. The dunes! The dunes were crucial to the stability of the beach. And tennis courts were a great idea. Good exercise before hitting the beach with the booze and the butts. Had to put an end to those low flying military jets too, pilots with their stiff erections

185

blasting across the broken-blue skies of his island. Didn't they realize they were ruining it for everyone, for chrissakes.

He ran the paper for three years, but was fading away. His writing "was wearing very thin," he admitted. He'd lost it. He sold the paper to some local boys (did he or didn't he? Addled reels the mind), promising he, and his buddies, would toss a piece or two their way just for old time's sake. "Beyond that," he wrote, "[I am] as dead as so many dinosaurs. It may be just as well."

Gibbs died on Fire Island.

Elinor found him dead in bed, an advance copy of his latest book open on his chest, a cigarette dangling between his fingers. It's been said that the doctor faked an autopsy because Elinor was afraid it was a suicide, but, of course, who knows.

Wolcott Gibbs was gone. He was 56.

John O'Hara remarked, "...he is all the proof you need that things do not even up in the end. They never evened up for him." Where it all ended knows God.

At least Fire Island had made him happy. He loved this goddam island.

Wolcott Gibbs (March 15, 1902 – August 16, 1958)

FRANK O'HARA – POETRY AND DEATH ON FIRE ISLAND

Frank O'Hara was a poet whose life, and tragic death, are inextricably bound with Fire Island.

O'Hara was an influential member of what has come to be known as The New York School, a group of poets, writers, artists, and musicians who were active in the 1950s and 60s. The movement included poets John Ashberry, Kenneth Koch, James Schuyler and Frank O'Hara among others. Artists included Jane Freilicher, Fairfield Porter, Grace Hartigan and Larry Rivers. Some of the musicians in the movement included John Cage, Morton Feldman, Earle Brown, Ned Rorem, and Christian Wolf.

COLLECTED POEMS OF FRANK O'HARA

EARLY DAYS

O'Hara's initial artistic inclination was toward music. He studied at the New England Conservatory in Boston where he developed into a proficient piano player. He joined the Navy during WWII and then, taking advantage of the GI Bill, went to Harvard where he began publishing poems, changing his major from music to English.

After obtaining his Masters from the University of Michigan graduate school, he moved to Greenwich Village in NYC and began teaching at the New School. As an aside, he got a job selling post cards at the Museum of Modern Art (MOMA), eventually working his way up to Assistant Curator of Painting and Sculptures Exhibits—a position that provided him with considerable influence.

As curator, he was in the rare position to introduce artists in one genre to those in others. He developed a personal affinity for painters becoming friends with Jackson Pollock, Willem de Kooning Franz Kline and Lee Krasner of the Abstract Expressionist movement. His Irish charm, affability, warmth and passion enabled him to make hundreds of friends, and enjoy a lengthy string of male lovers.

THE NEW YORK MOVEMENT

O'Hara was known as "a poet among painters," a poet who created poem paintings. He wrote of the mingling of these artists in the New York Movement in a memoir. "We were all in our early twenties...being poets, divid[ing] our time between the literary bar, the San Remo, and the artists' bar, the Cedar Tavern. In the San Remo we argued and gossiped: in the Cedar we often wrote poems while listening to the painters argue and gossip. . . the painters were the only generous audience for our poetry, and most of us read first publicly in art galleries or at The Club. The literary establishment cared about as much for our work as the Frick [art museum] cared for Pollock."

:O'HARA PLAQUE

There were numerous collaborations between members of the group. Grace Hartigan did twelve paintings for twelve O'Hara poems. Rivers and O'Hara combined lithographs with poems. The collaborative piece *"Stones"* was a book of lithographic prints by Rivers with poems by O'Hara. Composer Ned Rorem and O'Hara produced the piece "Dialogues for Two Voices and Two Pianos." He even made a movie with the painter Alfred Leslie, shared collages with Goldberg, comics with Joe

189

Brainard, and was the subject of paintings, both nude and not.

This was a creative time for all. Many were homosexual, including O'Hara who had a long time affair with Larry Rivers. Rivers married twice, fathered four children, and was involved with four other women during his life. This did not, however, stop him from engaging in a homosexual relationship with O'Hara.

Rivers wrote about the gay life, "…queerdom was a country in which there was more fun. There was something about homosexuality that seemed too much, too gorgeous, too ripe. I later came to realize that there was something marvelous about it because it seemed to be pushing everything to its fullest point.

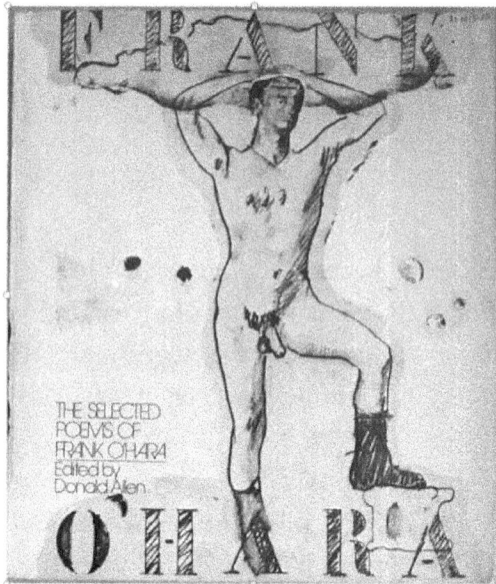

COVER OF COLLECTED WORKS OF FRANK O'HARA

Larry Rivers. *Cover for Collected Works of Frank O'Hara*, 1972 (collage) © 2021 Larry Rivers Foundation / VAGA at Artists Rights Society (ARS), NY by David Joel

O'Hara was strictly gay, courting numerous lovers, but Rivers seems to have been the individual with whom he most connected. Rivers painted O'Hara nude, clad only in black combat boots (one of his most renown works), but he also found O'Hara's attention stifling. O'Hara made demands that Rivers felt unreasonable. After one particular party, O'Hara wanted to go home with Rivers but Rivers thought otherwise. "He [O'Hara] thought he wasn't putting pressure on me but he actually was. Like we'd be somewhere and I'd be enjoying myself. And he says, 'Well, are we going?' Like meaning, 'Well is anything going to happen?' I wasn't in love in that sense."

THE POET EMERGES

O'Hara wrote his poems on the go, on his lunch break, on the ferry, in his office, alone or in rooms full of people. The painter John Button observed: "When asked by a publisher-friend for a book, Frank might have trouble even finding the poems stuffed into kitchen drawers or packed in boxes that had not been unpacked since his last move."

Fellow poet, John Ashbery claims he witnessed O'Hara, "Dashing the poems off at odd moments…he would then put them away in drawers and cartons and half forget them." O'Hara called this his, "I do this. I do that" poems, insisting that poetry should be "between two persons instead of two pages."

Early in his career, two volumes—*Second Avenue* (1960) and *Lunch Poems* (1965)—were in print. His books were printed in editions of only hundreds of copies. It was not until after his death that the plethora of his work was discovered. International acclaim followed.

Take this reading of his poem "A Step Away From Them" from his collection published as "Lunch Poems:"

"It's my lunch hour, so I go
for a walk among the hum-colored
cabs. First, down the sidewalk
where laborers feed their dirty
glistening torsos sandwiches
and Coca-Cola...

A Negro stands in a doorway with a
toothpick, languorously agitating.
A blonde chorus girl clicks: he
smiles and rubs his chin. Everything
suddenly honks: it is 12:40 of
a Thursday."

Here is another, this from the poem "Mayakovsky" in the 1957 Grove Press edition of "Meditations in an Emergency," read by Dan Drapper on the TV show "Mad Men:"

"...Now I am quietly waiting for
the catastrophe of my personality
to seem beautiful again,
and interesting, and modern."

One purpose of poetry is to awaken the mind, like a bugle, from its superficial stupor of selfness—to make one ask, "Huh?"

Take *just* the title of his poem on the passing of Billie Holiday "The Day Lady Died."

Published as "Lady Day Died," the title would be merely expository. OK, Lady Day (Billie Holiday) died. Alternatively, the title could have read "The Day Lady Day Died" but that is too much like a newspaper headline.

Change the title to "The Day Lady Died" and the reader is asking, "What lady? Huh?"However, we know what lady, Lady Day. O'Hara adds the final line, *"...and everyone and I stopped breathing,"* cementing the sentiment.

This is his genius. In his "Poem Read at Joan Mitchell's," from a series of *Odes* (1960) he wrote*: "tonight I feel energetic because I'm sort of the bugle, / like waking people up. . . ."* There's that bugle again!

DEATH FORETOLD?

Perhaps no poem captures O'Hara's talent better than "A True Account of Talking to the Sun at Fire Island," arguably one of his finest poems. It was written in answer to the poem "An Extraordinary Adventure Which Befell Vladimir Mayakovsky in a Summer Cottage," by the Russian poet Mayakovsky, one of O'Hara's favorites. It appears to foretell O'Hara's own death.

Frank was heading home after a night partying in Fire Island Pines in the company of J.J. Mitchell. He was drunk and tired. The beach taxi in which they were traveling blew a tire stranding them on the dark beach to await the arrival of a rescue taxi. It was 2:40 AM.

Mitchell and the other passengers gathered on the dune side of the vehicle while Frank wandered off toward the ocean. A local 23-year-old with his girlfriend was heading for a club in Cherry Grove in an old jeep when Frank appeared out of the darkness directly in front of the jeep.

It hit him head-on.

Frank sustained massive injuries, a broken leg, broken ribs and a lacerated liver. He was transported to a local hospital where he lingered for two days before dying. O'Hara was 40 years old.

Larry Rivers delivered a eulogy as poignant as Alfred Leslie's paintings, "The Killing Cycle." Painted poems—again.

While going through O'Hara's effects, fellow poet Kenneth Koch came across "A True Account of Talking to the Sun at Fire Island," the poem O'Hara had written in answer to Mayakovsky sun poem. It had been written July 10, 1958, eight years earlier, not far from where he was killed. Almost prophetically, its final stanza talks about his death.

> *"Sun, don't go!" I was awake*
> *at last. "No, go I must, they're calling*
> *me."*
> *"Who are they?"*
>
> *Rising he said "Some*
> *day you'll know. They're calling to you*
> *too." Darkly he rose, and then I slept.*

THEN AND NOW

Introduction: With our eye on FIN's 60 Anniversary, we sent History columnist Tom McGann a well-worn vintage copy of Fire Island News to get his perspective on what has changed and what remains the same on our beloved Fire Island. His insights might surprise you. We thank Ocean Beach Historical Society for their assistance with this project.

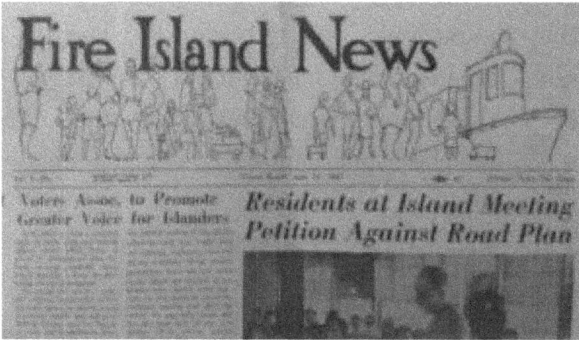

The June 17, 1961 edition of Fire Island News paints a portrait of life on Fire Island as seen by Dali. The island is both easily recognizable and distorted at the same time. Though printed only in black and white type back then, color still manages to shimmer from those newspaper pages published so many decades ago, words bringing history alive.

The frame is intact (the familiar Fire Island News logo remains largely unchanged), and, news being news, politics dominates the front page. RESIDENTS AT

ISLAND MEETING PETITION AGAINST ROAD PLAN reads the headline.

One might yawn at such old news, after all the fight against Robert Moses' plan to build a road the length of Fire Island was won way back in 1964, but to the residents who attended that meeting it was an uncertain future that yawned before them – vague and ugly – the same devious politics we continue to witness to this very day.

The Islip Town Supervisor at the time, Thomas Harwood, lied (as politicians are wont to do) about the purpose of a proposed right of way from Kismet to Ocean Beach. Its purpose was only for the use by emergency vehicles he insisted. One resident's objection to "a road from nowhere to nowhere" was met with cheers. Those who fought the fight can still hear the echoes of those cheers today.

A sister piece to that article, also on the front page, describes the progress being made on the $10 million dollar Fire Island Bridge that would join Long Island to Fire Island. Its completion date was scheduled for April 1964.

In one of history's ironic twists of fate, the Fire Island Bridge became part of the causeway named after Robert Moses. Today, the Robert Moses Causeway ends right where the road he planned down Fire Island was to begin—the road never built.

In opposition to the overwhelming sentiments of Fire Island residents, on the editorial page, under the paper's masthead, the publishers came out in favor of the Kismet to Ocean Beach right of way. They then played both sides against the middle, noting that "no argument, no matter how strong, can stand up to the logicality of connecting two dead-end bridges." They then encouraged all residents to join the newly formed Fire Island Voters Association in order to defeat the proposed Robert Moses road.

The publishers would change their minds over the intervening years and come out strongly against that road, but this editorial shows how tangled the situation was in June of '61. You can almost smell the sweat in the newsroom as they struggled with this problem, an issue that only became even more strident until the establishment of the Fire Island National Seashore put an end to any plans for any roads.

Also on the editorial page was a News reprint entitled "Parental Responsibility" that seems oddly out of place in today's world. Apparently, large groups of teenagers descended on Cherry Grove and the Pines the previous Memorial Day for a few hours of "wild fun … drinking, necking [a 1961 colloquial term meaning making out, kissing, whatever], and disorderly conduct."

The editorial goes on to rebuke any teenager who would "drink himself into a stupor, smash windows, tear up a garden, or prove his manliness by beating up homosexuals." The latitude of deference expressed here is mind boggling given the advances made by the LBGTQ community. One can barely imagine conduct such as this occurring on Fire Island today.

The following pages describe house fires and a tragic local drowning, occurrences still all too frequent, still being documented today.

Then there is the story about 38 gold pieces found by one Benjamin Shalott as he made his rounds along the beach during the War of 1812. Stories of buried treasure on Fire Island are common, and, in some cases, accurate. Just as in yesteryear, the mere whisper of a new cache of gold doubloons buried somewhere on the beach is sure to bring out droves of treasure hunters armed with today's most advanced metal detectors, delivered just yesterday by Amazon.

There are Letters to the Editor (the subjects remain the same, only the names of the authors differ), Calendar of Events (same events, different years), Directory of Services (service guide to doctors, lawyers, fire chiefs, builders, boaters, bars and more. The latest edition lists the names of the grandsons and/or granddaughters of those posted in '61).

Then as now, there is the ever-popular Police Blotter. The recurrent crimes remain the same.

Since the inception of Fire Island News, each community has the opportunity to express "what's happening" in a column dedicated strictly to itself. Depending on who is counting and what they consider a town, the number of communities along the island varies somewhere around 16. Of these, usually 8 to 10 publish columns regularly. It is not surprising that most of the concerns are environmental and continue to be discussed year after year.

Gala parties are also headlined as couples vie to be the most admired. Time marches on and a couple's 50th anniversary too soon becomes their 75th.

There is usually a restaurant review, usually positive, usually spotlighting some restaurant new to the island. Gone are the Sea Turtle, and the Sea Shack, the

Sandpiper (not the one we know today), John & Anne's, Goldies, and numerous Bayviews.

Sailor's Haven even advertised their Seafarer's Bar and nightclub entertainment unaware that they would be transformed into a National Park Service facility only five years later. But some restaurants have weathered Fire Island's many storms, weather-wise and other-wise: Maguire's, Flynn's, Kismet Inn, the Casino, Blue Whale and a small handful of others—a small handful indeed.

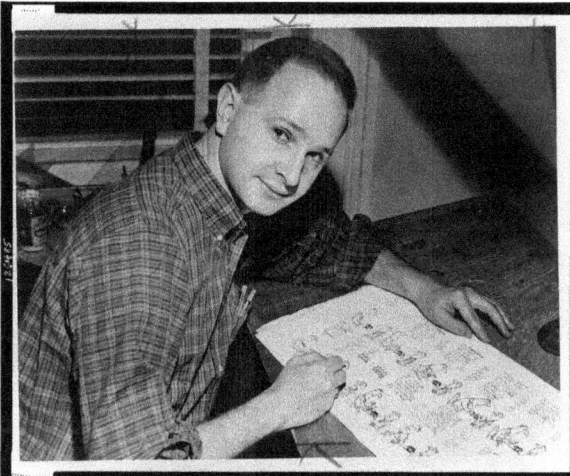

JULES FEIFFER AT WORK ON CARTOON
Picryl Public Domain

But one thing is missing and can, probably, never be replaced. Jules Feiffer published his pointed, political cartoon satires each week, an addition that gave Fire Island News Greenwich Village-cred, a sophistication welcomed by its readers. It is no more and, Jules, we miss you.

And so it goes. The more things change the more they remain the same, faithfully documented by Fire Island News, then and now.

MAURICE "WHERE THE WILD THINGS ARE TAMED" SENDAK
Live Your Life

Maurice Sendak was a Fire Islander, the author of the 1964 Caldecott Award winning children's book "Where the Wild Things Are." The book remains number three on the top ten bestselling children's books of all time. You may have read it yourself. If not, it is not too late—yet. Are you ready? Are you ready? Are you ready?

BACKGROUND:

The basics of Sendak's life are well documented so only a brief summary is necessary here. He was born in Brooklyn in 1928 to Polish, Jewish immigrant parents, the youngest of three siblings. He was a sickly child, exposed early in life to the concept of mortality by deaths of family members during the Holocaust. Many of his books contain tracings of fences and towers and walls of concentration camps.

At the age of twelve he saw Walt Disney's *Fantasia* and decided to become an illustrator. In fact, Sendak so loved Disney that he has the second most extensive collection of Walt Disney memorabilia, second only to Walt's own daughter. Upon graduation from the New York Art Students League he worked as a window dresser in the famous children's toy store F.A.O. Schwartz, but soon obtained commissions to illustrate Marcel Ayme's *The Wonderful Farm* and Ruth Krauss's *A Hole is to Dig*. He was on his way.

The first book both written and illustrated by Sendak was *Kenny's Window* (1956), followed by his four-volume *Nutshell Library* (1962). Perhaps his most ambitious endeavor was his trilogy based on the psychological development of children. First he wrote *Where the Wild Things Are* (1963) aimed at pre-school kids. Then came *In the Night Kitchen* (1970) for toddlers, and, finally, *Outside over There* (1981) for pre-adolescents.

In the Night Kitchen was number 24 on the "100 Most Frequently Banned/Challenged Books of 2000-2009" for its depictions of a boy about three years old cavorting about with his pee-pee showing. For a perspective, the Harry Potter books rank number one on that same list.

In all Sendak produced over 50 books, including illustrating *The Velveteen Rabbit*.

In 1975 he expanded his horizons into television by writing and directing an animated special titled "Really Rosie." He collaborated with Carole King to turn it into a musical play in 1978.

With seemingly unlimited talent, Sendak also had a successful career as a stage designer for operas by Mozart, Prokofiev, and Ravel. He even staged Tchaikovsky's *Nutcracker*.

SENDAK AND FIRE ISLAND:

Sendak took a house on Fire Island with his companion/lover Eugene Glynn in the early 1960s, and wrote *Where the Wild Things Are* (WTWTA) while living on "B Walk" in Seaview. His neighbors, and fellow *bon vivants*, were Amos & Marcia Vogel, and Nat & Margo Hentoff.

THE HOUSE SENDAK LIVED IN ON FIRE ISLAND
Courtesy of Robert Sherman

"They often met on the beach, where Sendak would sit for hours, sketching," recalled the Vogel's son, Loring. The young Loring Vogel was the protagonist of a book collaboration authored by Loring's father and illustrated by Sendak entitled *How Little Lori Visited Times Square*. Copies of the book can still be purchased today.

Sendak was a humanist, ribald while also conservative with a European sensibility. He wore a suit and tie even while championing the pleasure principle, the gratification of needs. Amos Vogel was the founder of the NYC avant-garde Cinema 16, famous for introducing new films by up-and-coming directors such as Roman Polanski, John Cassavetes, and Alan Resnais. Nat Hentoff was a columnist for *The Village Voice* in NYC from 1958-2009, a staff writer for *The New Yorker*, and, perhaps, the preeminent jazz critic of his time. These three couples called themselves the "Nintimates," hedonists of the early '60s, known for their love of freedom, fun and laughter.

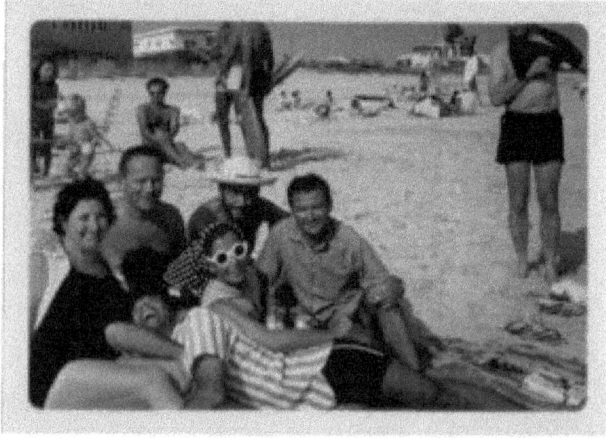
THE VOGELS, THE HENTOFFS AND SENDAK
Courtesy of Loring Vogel

SENDAK AND WORK:

From journeyman to consummate artist, Sendak took great pains with each of his works. Originally, WTWTA was entitled "Where the Wild Horses Are." The problem was that Sendak could not draw horses. His editor, Ursula Nordstrom, asked him in "acid tones" what could he draw. His response was "things," so "things" it became.

Sendak did not consider his books to be children's books. In a piece in *The New Yorker* he stated, "Kid's books...Grownup books...That's just marketing. Books are Books."

He married the relationship between illustrations and words thusly: "Words are left out—but the picture says it. Pictures are left out—but the word says it." His illustrations, he said, are "all a kind of caricatures of me. They look as if they'd been hit on the head, and hit so hard they weren't going to grow anymore...I am trying to draw the way children *feel*—or, rather, the way I imagine they feel. It's the way *I know* I felt as a child."

He loved music; was obsessed with Mozart. "I wanted at all costs to avoid the serious pitfall of illustrating with pictures what the author had already…illustrated with words. I hoped, rather, to let the story speak for itself, with my pictures as a kind of background music—music in the right style and always in tune with the words." True to his word, he drew and painted to music, trying always to find the right piece to fit the mood of his work. And he drew and listened, listened and drew, drew and listened.

He did not write for children per se. "I really do these books for myself. It's something I have to do, find it's the only thing I want to do. Reaching the kids is important, but secondary. First, always, I have to reach and keep hold of the child in me."

THE BUNGALOW WHERE SENDAK WORKED
Courtesy of Robert Sherman

SENDAK AND CHILDREN:

Maurice loved children. His editor Nordstrom once said, "[S]omehow Maurice has retained a direct line to his own childhood." Maurice was their champion, dealing directly and honestly with them. He protected the sanctity of children's feelings even though he remembered his own childhood with some trepidation. Some characters in WTWTA are representations of his relatives with their yellow teeth and wild hair who came to visit, pulling at him, pinching him and eating all his food. "In reality, childhood is deep and rich. It's vital, mysterious, and profound. I remember my own childhood vividly...I knew terrible things, but I knew I mustn't let adults know I knew...it would scare them."

And: "You can't protect kids. They know everything."

And: "My childhood self...as if it were all quaint and succulent like Peter Pan. Childhood is cannibals and psychotics vomiting in your mouth."

While many adults found his stories and pictures of beasts frightening, the children had no such fears. Somehow Sendak tamed these "wild things." A seven-year-old boy once wrote him a letter in which he wrote, "How much does it cost to get to where the wild things are? If it is not too expensive my sister and I want to spend the summer there. Please answer soon."

In spite of the grotesque, he touched a nerve in children. "A little boy sent me a charming card with a little drawing on it. I loved it. I answer all my children's letters—sometimes very hastily—but this one I lingered over. I sent him a card and I drew a picture of a Wild Thing on it. I wrote, 'Dear Jim: I loved your card.' Then I got a letter back from his mother and she said: 'Jim loved your card so much he ate it.' That to me was one of the highest compliments

I've ever received. He didn't care that it was an original Maurice Sendak drawing or anything. He saw it, he loved it, he ate it."

SENDAK ON DEATH:

Although Sendak was an atheist and did not believe in an afterlife, he fully believed that he would see his dead brother again. He also sighed that a belief in God "must have made life much easier. It's harder for us non-believers."

"I have nothing now but praise for my life. I'm not unhappy. I cry a lot because I miss people. They die and I can't stop them. They leave me and I love them more...What I dread is the isolation...There are so many beautiful things in the world which I will have to leave when I die, but I'm ready, I'm ready, I'm ready."

"It is a blessing to get old, to find the time to read the books, to listen to the music...I will cry my way all the way to the grave...Live your life. Live your life. Live your life."

Sendak died in Danbury, CT on May 8, 2012, shortly before his 84th birthday. His body was cremated.

A BRIEF HISTORY OF MAGUIRE'S
RESTAURANT, OCEAN BEACH

Courtesy of Jim Betz

The pride that residents of Fire Island harbor is sometimes overlooked, but it is hard to miss the obvious pride that the owners of Maguire's Bay Front Restaurant, Jim Betz and Drew Becker, demonstrate summer after summer. One look at their extensive renovations is proof positive.

Maguire's is one of the oldest restaurants on Fire Island, predated by the Surf Hotel of 1855 (since demolished) and the Perkinson's Restaurant in Cherry Grove, 1868 (later Duffy's Hotel, destroyed by fire in 1956.) The building was originally the clubhouse of the Ocean Beach Yacht Club, circa 1926, a "Men Only" club.

In 1935 a man by the name of Frank Maguire won the Irish Sweepstakes. According to the newspaper *The*

Brooklyn Daily Eagle, Maguire knew he had won but did not know how much. "Say that again," he said. When he was told the amount, $75, 250 dollars ($1.3 million today), he replied, "That'll hold me."

With his winnings he hired an LIRR passenger train and took his friends out to Montauk. With the rest of the money he purchased the clubhouse in Ocean Beach and converted it into a public restaurant. The restaurant property had 235 feet of bay front, all fully bulkheaded, divided into 13 slips, two of which could accommodate boats up to 50' in length. Frank Maguire ran the restaurant until 1939 when he leased it to John Flynn of Ocean Bay Park for ten years.

Jack Flynn leased Maguire's in Ocean Beach in 1939, and gave it to his son, Frank, to run in '42 after Frank returned from the war. Frank Flynn did so well that Maguire wanted the restaurant back and refused to renew the lease. Flynn returned to OPB and the family began expanding their businesses there.

In 1949 Frank Maguire took back the restaurant (then named "Flynns") hoping to ride its swell of success, and changed the name back to "Maguire's". The business suffered and after he died his wife Leila married a retired NYC fireman, William Gal, to help her run the place, but by then the task proved too difficult. She put the property up for sale in 1966 insisting on $235,000, a thousand dollars for each foot of bay front property. There were no buyers.

That same year three recent graduates of the U.S. Coast Guard Academy, Tom Keeney, Tom McGann and Larry Dallaire, started a successful water ski school out of one of the slips behind Maguire's Restaurant. At the end of the '66 season, having no buyers for her property, Mrs. Gal extended the offer to Tom, Tom and Larry. They had no money but they jumped at the opportunity. They signed a ten year lease with an option to buy and were given until the Spring of 1967 to come up with the down payment.

With the Viet Nam war in full force, the three joined the Merchant Marine and shipped out to earn some much needed money. By spring they had the cash, but no experience in the restaurant business except as patrons. By dint of hours of study, hard work, and dedication they managed to turn the once-failing business around and keep it afloat.

Noting the upswing in business, one summer afternoon the Mayor and one of the Trustees (both of whom shall remain nameless) sat on the restaurant's then tiny 10' x 10' deck for a discussion on what plans the boys had in mind. They outlined their idea to build a "T" pier out into the bay with a clam bar on its end. They also planned to build a boatel on the vacant property next to the restaurant to accommodate additional guests.

At the next town board meeting the Mayor and the Trustees condemned Maguire's bay front, securing it for the village. They also passed an ordinance that no new multi-unit dwellings would be permitted to be built in Ocean Beach. The village pumped in some sand and called the condemned property the "baby beach." There no longer is a "baby beach" as the sand has long since been swept away by the tides.

The boys shipped out again the following winter, earning extra money by signing up for hazardous duty pay transporting ammunition into the war zone. Shortly after they returned, Mrs. Gal passed away.

The boys intended to close the restaurant for a day in memory of Mrs. Gal, but her stepson told them that his mother would not want the restaurant closed. Instead, the restaurant remained opened that day in celebration of her life.

The three sailors, turned restaurateurs, exercised their option to buy the property and decided some physical changes to the building were needed. The wall between the bar and the dining area was removed. The bar was moved to the northeast corner of the dining room and doubled in size. They introduced a lobster tank and when the 1968 season ended they had quadrupled their gross.

Since plans for their boatel had been thwarted, the boys floated over three houses from West Island and placed them on the vacant property adjacent to the restaurant.

In 1969 Maguire's was the headquarters of, and the caterers for, the production company filming the movie *Last Summer* on Fire Island. It starred Academy Award Nominee Catherine Burns, Barbara Hersey, Richard Thomas, and Bruce Davidson. The Academy Award nominated team of Frank Perry, and his wife Eleanor Perry (*David and Lisa*) were the director and screenwriter respectively.

Marriage plans were in the offing and new business ventures beckoned, so the boys decided to sell the business. George Bockhart, their chef was first choice. George selected a friend Max Schlitter to be his partner. George and Max took over in the summer of 1970, continuing to build on the restaurant's success. Max ran the front end while George continued to prepare the delicious food for which Maguire's had become famous.

GEORGE AND MAX
Photo courtesy of George Bockhart

They purchased the real estate in 1986, and made several renovations to increase the efficiency and appeal of the restaurant. In total, George and Max ran Maguire's for 25 years, before selling to Jim Betz and Drew Becker in 1995.

These present proprietors infused youthful enthusiasm and continuing efforts to increase the quality of the meals and the service provided. But they did not have it easy. Flooding of the town was a growing threat, and several storms wreaked havoc on Fire Island.

While George and Max had to suffer through "The Perfect Storm," (Halloween of '91), no one anticipated the damage hurricane Sandy—the "Frankenstorm"—would inflict, not just on Fire Island, but on the entire eastern seaboard.

Jim and Drew not only bounced back from Superstorm Sandy, pumping untold dollars into Maguire's to restore it, but spent even more money to enhance the look and efficiency of the restaurant. They went so far as to completely redo the lavatories to comply with the

213

American with Disabilities Act. This is the kind of pride demonstrated by the past and present owners of Maguire's who have gone out of their way to provide a first class restaurant for the community.

And it shows.

DREW & JIM
Courtesy of Jim Betz

Over the years numerous celebrities have dined at Maguire's. Fanny Brice (think *Funny Girl*) was a frequent guest in the late '30s and early '40. Other stage and screen celebrities were Mel Brooks and Ann Bancroft, Woody Allen, Tony Randall, Patty Duke, Steve Buscemi, Tony Roberts; musicians Meatloaf, Alice Cooper; sports figures Joe Namath, middle weight boxing champion Rocky (*Somebody Up There Likes Me*) Graziano, Pele, Frank Gifford; the famous '60s painter Peter Max and untold others from various professions.

Numerous musical acts have also appeared at Maguire's. Some of the more notable are Taj Mahal, Ivan Neville, Big Sam's Funky Nation, George Porter Jr., Cyril

Neville, Eric Lindell, Dragon Smoke, the Mojo Rhythm Kings, Tab Benoit, and more.

Such dedication to the community needs to be recognized and applauded.

MARTIN LUTHER KING, JR. AND FIRE ISLAND

On September 2, 1967 Nobel Peace Prize recipient Dr. Martin Luther King Jr. was the guest of honor at a fund raiser in Seaview, Fire Island.

WITH PRESIDENT LYNDON JOHNSON AT THE
SIGNING OF THE CIVIL RIGHTS ACT 1964

Despite the fact that the summer of '67 was called "the Summer of Love," the country was in the midst of political and cultural turmoil. While Scott Mackenzie was singing "San Francisco (Be Sure to Wear Flowers in Your Hair)," Dr. King was engaged in a fight for the civil rights of African-Americans.

All of what you will read here really happened. For those too young to remember this will just be a synoptic

217

history lesson. For those who lived it, it remains all too real.

Dr. King started early. In 1956, less than six months after receiving his PhD in Theology, he led the Montgomery Bus Boycott. It was in response to Rosa Parks' arrest for failure to give up her seat on a city bus to a white man. The resultant publicity catapulted him to the leadership of the civil rights movement.

Dr. King adopted a policy of non-violent civil disobedience, based on the philosophy of Mahatma Gandhi and Henry David Thoreau (a F.I. visitor himself). He led demonstrations, sit-ins, and voter registration drives to call attention to the plight of African-Americans.

To give you a sense of those times, in 1956 the average cost of a new car was $2100, and a gallon of gas cost 24 cents. The Dow Jones Average hit a new all time high just over 500. "I Love Lucy" was the number one TV show, and "Heartbreak Hotel" by Elvis Presley was the top single (back then records were sold individually as 45 rpm 7 inch discs.)

On August 28, 1963 Dr. King led the historic March on Washington attended by an estimated 250,000 people. The event culminated in his "I Have a Dream" speech, heralded as among the finest in American history.

A scant three months later, President John F. Kennedy, a fierce warrior for civil rights, was assassinated. The new President, Lyndon Johnson, called upon Congress for passage of the Civil Rights Act of 1964 to honor Kennedy's memory. But it was not going to be quite that easy as a tumultuous battle for passage of the bill was underway in both houses of Congress. Dr. King had swayed public opinion in favor of the act, and that, coupled with sentiment for the recently slain JFK, finally facilitated passage of the bill.

DR. KING WASHINGTON D.C. I HAVE A DREAM
SPEECH

In recognition of the magnitude of his achievements, Dr. King was presented with the Nobel Peace Prize. In his acceptance speech he spoke about the power of non-violence—even in the face of violence.

Western culture was undergoing seismic changes. Men grew their hair long while skirt lengths shortened. The Beatles turned rock and roll music on its head with the release of "Sgt. Pepper's Lonely Hearts Club Band." Pot smoking became endemic. "Turn on, tune in, drop out" became a catch phrase as experimentation with drugs expanded to include the use of LSD, mushrooms and other psychedelic substances. Fire Island, where Dr. King would soon visit, was in the vanguard of these changes.

The war in Viet Nam was escalating. Between 1964 and 1973 in excess of 2 million young men—men only—were drafted. More than 58,000 were killed in action. Opposition to the war was high. Demonstrators invaded university campuses. Draft cards were burned. Men ran off to Canada. Some were arrested and jailed.

Dr. King decided to expand his mission to include ending the war in Viet Nam, much to the chagrin of some of his most ardent supporters. He also promoted open housing, and organized a Poor People's Campaign for economic justice.

In response to acts of violence against those attempting to register voters—both black and white activists had been murdered—demonstrators marched from Selma, Alabama to its capital Montgomery in March '65 where Dr. King delivered his "How Long Not Long" speech affirming that equal rights were close "because the arc of the moral universe is long, but it bends toward justice."

Then on September 2, 1967, while most Fire Islanders were going about their business unaware of history in the making, Dr. King arrived on Fire Island as a guest of John Morrin. At a rally in Seaview, Dr. King spoke about community, the war in Vietnam, anti-Semitism and the need for a third political party. After the rally a cocktail party was held in Ocean Bay Park, at the home of Mr. and Mrs. Hyman Abbot, where $4000 was raised ($30,000 in today's money).

In spite of the fact that posters had been torn down throughout the community, the gathering was still attended by over 1,500 people. It elicited responses from the predominantly white audience such as, "Tell them, brother, tell them." Authors Herman Wouk and Bel Kaufman were in attendance, and both expressed enthusiasm upon hearing the civil rights leader speak, but were dismayed regarding the poor reception from some residents. Kaufman was quoted in the New York Times on September 4, 1967 saying "The people you would like to reach are never the ones who show up at meetings."

Michael Abbott of Ocean Bay Park remembers that Dr. King spoke to a large crowd of people gathered on the beach at K Street in Seaview and later attended the fund-raising cocktail party for SCLC. Dr. King spent the night at the Abbott home, and Michael, age 13 at the time, had breakfast with him the following morning.

Shortly thereafter, Dr. King, visiting Memphis, Tennessee in support of black sanitation workers, delivered his "I've Been to the Mountaintop" speech in which he addressed the numerous death threats he had been receiving.

"Well, I don't know what will happen now. We've got some difficult days ahead. But it doesn't matter with me now. Because I've been to the mountaintop. And I don't mind. Like anybody, I would like to live a long life. Longevity has its place. But I'm not concerned about that now. I just want to do God's will. And He's allowed me to go up to the mountain. And I've looked over. And I've seen the Promised Land. I may not get there with you. But I want you to know tonight, that we, as a people, will get to the Promised Land. So I'm happy, tonight. I'm not worried about anything. I'm not fearing any man. Mine eyes have seen the glory of the coming of the Lord."

Dr. King was assassinated the following day.

As an interesting historical aside, this little spit of land, Fire Island, has hosted two Nobel Peace Prize recipients. Both Dr. Martin Luther King, Jr. and General George C. Marshall have tread its sandy shores. Not many locales can claim such an honor.

MAYBE IT WAS JUST THE TIMES OR MAYBE IT WAS JUST TIME FOR A RIOT

STONEWALL REVOLUTION - IT WAS THE BEST OF TIMES, IT WAS THE WORST OF TIMES

THE STONEWALL INN

Who really knows why it all happened? Probably no one, not even those who were there. At least that's how the story of the Stonewall riots continues to be told.

The cascading events during those times boggle the mind: the Civil Rights Movement, (Dr. King assassinated), the Anti-War Movement (Yippies' heads bloodied in Chicago at the Democratic National Convention), the Viet Nam Tet Offensive (we won the battle but lost the war), Bobby Kennedy's assassination ("Now it's on to Chicago." He never made it). It was hard to keep up. History was unfolding at warp speed.

There was the mind-blowing music. The Beatles performed for the last time in an impromptu concert on a rooftop. Led Zeppelin played the blues like heavy metal. The Who released a rock opera called *Tommy*. Elvis had a triumphant come-back. *Hair* was a smash hit on Broadway issuing in the Age of Aquarius with nudity and hallucinogenic drugs. "Let the sun shine. Let the sunshine. Let the sun shine in."

Oh yeah—and man was about to walk on the moon. Plug that into your brain!

Sex and drugs and rock and roll. The times were just *so* crazy!

So, maybe it was just the times or maybe it was just time for a riot. Something was in the air that sweltering night at the Stonewall Inn in Greenwich Village, NYC, June 28, 1969.

Judy Garland had recently died and her funeral had taken place just hours before. Emotions were raw, but her death probably had nothing to do with what happened. No one knows but that argument lives on like a xeroxed zombie, and a spontaneous riot did erupt that night at the Stonewall Inn.

Not that the Stonewall Inn was much of a place. In 1966 the Mafia had turned two storefronts located at 51-53 Christopher Street into a gay bar frequented primarily by men. It had no running water behind the bar. Glasses were merely rinsed out in tubs of dirty water before being reused. The toilets were famous for overflowing and there were no fire exits. The place did not even have a liquor license and it was rumored that the booze was watered down. But none of that prevented the Stonewall Inn from becoming *the* gay bar in the city. Its big draw was that it was the only gay bar that permitted men to dance with other men, but that was enough.

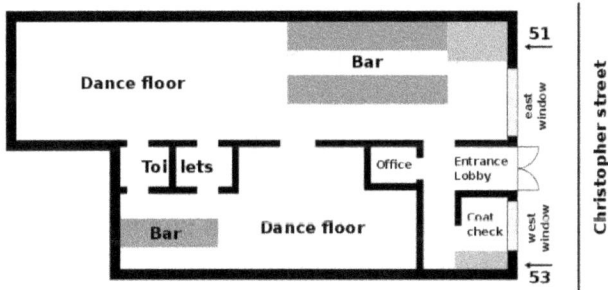

Dance floor

Bar

51

east window

Christopher street

Toilets

Office

Entrance Lobby

Bar

Dance floor

Coat check

west window

53

LAYOUT OF THE STONEWALL INN 1969
Licensed CC BY-SA 3.0

So, what happened and why? There are no definitive answers, but the consensus is that the NYC police, who raided the Stonewall Inn on a regular basis, confronted a crowd of about 200 who, though long accustomed to such raids, were in no mood to be manhandled that particular night.

Four cops, two in uniform and two supervisors showed up at 1:20 a.m. for a routine raid. Typically, the cops would segregate the transvestites from the rest of the crowd to check whether their gender matched their attire. Any men dressed as women, or women as men, would be arrested—but not that night.

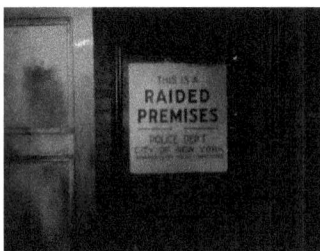

STONEWALL INN GETS RAIDED

The drag queens refused to be searched, and other patrons refused to show their IDs. The compliant were sent packing. According to a long-time bartender who is still alive, a priest escaped secreted in the crowd.

But instead of going home the crowds remained outside the bar and started ridiculing the police. Bystanders joined in and the size of the crowd grew. Estimates ranged from a few hundred to a thousand.

Good-natured high jinks heightened the general amusement and good humor of the crowd. Exaggerated poses and street performances were egged on by the applause of the gathering throng. The crowd threw mock salutes at the members of the "Public Morals Squad."

The police handcuffed those arrested and escorted them out to the waiting paddy wagon. When the cops went in to bring others out the first prisoners escaped. It was like a circus act featuring Keystone Kops, but the act had an underlying uneasiness, an edge of anger and latent hostility.

A "stone-cold dyke" in handcuffs scuffled with the police until one cop hit her with a billy club. As she was being thrown into the paddy wagon, she yelled at the crowd, "Why don't you guys do something?" The crowd went berserk and started throwing bottles, rocks, bricks, anything they could get their hands on. Homeless, gay, street kids led the attack.

A group of cops drove off for reinforcements while others barricaded themselves inside the tavern. The "fairies" had finally had enough. They rebelled.

A parking meter was liberated and used as a battering ram against the locked Stonewall's doors. Garbage cans were set afire and tossed against the building. Windows were smashed. Burning garbage was stuffed through the broken windows into the bar. The cops broke out a fire hose but they could not get it up and operating because of a lack of water pressure.

The Tactical Police Force (TPF) finally arrived equipped with full-face helmets and truncheons. To the tune of "Ta-ra-ra-Boom-de-ray," the mocking mob broke out in a spur-of-the-moment kick-line singing "We are the Stonewall girls/ We wear our hair in curls/ We don't wear underwear/ We show our pubic hair/And wear our dungarees/above our nelly knees."

The cops moved forward in a wedge formation to clear the area. Another kick-line was formed. Another police wedge. Kick-line. Wedge.

The riots continued until four a.m. and resumed the following night. They continued until Wednesday when the crowd advanced on the offices of the *Village Voice*— perhaps the most liberal newspaper in NY—threatening to burn it down because of its demeaning coverage of the rebellion and name-calling: "forces of faggotry," "limp wrists," "Sunday fag follies."

An eye witness said: "The cops were totally humiliated...the fairies were not supposed to riot...no group had ever forced the cops to retreat before, so the anger was enormous." The police wrote the incident up as an "unusual occurrence."

The *NY Daily News* ran a blatantly offensive headline: "Homo Nest Raided, Queen Bees Are Stinging Mad." The *NY Times* tucked a small column somewhere deep in the paper, but at least the world began to pay attention to LBGTQ rights.

The Beat poet, Allen Ginsberg (*Howl*) wrote: "You know, the guys there were so beautiful—they've lost that wounded look that fags all had 10 years ago."

On the one year anniversary NYC held Christopher Street Liberation Day, sister parades were held in Los Angeles and Chicago, the first gay pride parades in U.S. history. The following year there were parades in six major U.S. cities as well as in four international capitals: London, Paris, West Berlin and Stockholm.

Unfortunately, the Stonewall Inn itself only lasted six months after the riots. For years it was home to assorted businesses before reopening as a gay establishment in the late 1990s. It underwent major renovations in 2007 and is now fully operational paying homage to its rich heritage.

In 2000 the Stonewall Inn was designated a National Historic Landmark, and in 2016 President Obama announced the establishment of the Stonewall National

Monument, including Christopher Street and the inn. It is the first and, as now, only LBGTQ national monument.

A mere three weeks before the 50th anniversary of the Stonewall rebellion, Thursday, June 6, 2019, NYPD Commissioner James O'Neill apologized to the LBGTQ community stating, "The actions taken by the NYPD were wrong—plain and simple. The actions and laws were discriminatory and oppressive, and, for that, I apologize."

On Fire Island the Cherry Grove Community House and Theater has been listed on the National Register of Historic Places because of its intimate connection with LBGTQ history.

CHERRY GROVE COMMUNITY HOUSE AND THEATER
Courtesy of Leah Fallica CC BY-SA 4.0

The Stonewall rebellion is the birthday of Gay Liberation, the celebration of gender nonconformity.

Remember Judy Garland? "Somewhere over the rainbow skies are blue, where the dreams that you dare to dream really do come true." Miraculous!

LAMBDA LEGAL – PROTECTING
LBGT RIGHTS FOR 45 YEARS

Lambda Legal is a civil rights organization that specializes in lesbian, bisexual, gay, transgender and queer (LBGTQ) rights, as well as those living with AIDS/HIV.

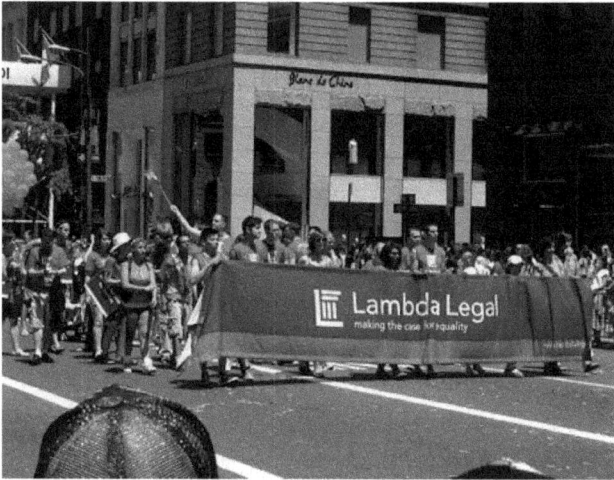

Courtesy of Lambda Legal

In 1971, Lambda Legal's founder William J. Thom, was sitting around a pool in the Fire Island Pines lamenting the frequent arrests of local gay men. Jack Lichtenstein, a straight lawyer who had often taken his own boat across the bay to bail out those arrested, suggested that an organization be formed to protect gay rights. Thom picked up the ball and submitted **nonprofit** incorporation papers to the New York courts. **Lambda Legal became its own first client when the** application was denied on the grounds that its proposed activities would be contrary to public policy, i.e. its mission was "neither benevolent nor charitable."

Undaunted, Thom appealed to New York's highest court and the court finally ruled in his favor, allowing it to become a non-profit organization. Lambda Legal considers its date of incorporation as 10/18/73, marking nearly 50 years of hard fought battles for LBGTQ rights.

The three original leaders of Lambda Legal were Bill Thom, E. Carrington Boggan and Michael Lavery. In 1974 the first woman, Nathalie Rockhill was elected to the board. She, among others, had founded the National Gay Task Force, the first national gay rights group in America. As a major figure in the post Stonewall days, her move to Lambda Legal was warmly welcomed and by the 1980s men and women were equally represented on the board of directors.

Since 1973 the few who volunteered their time has now expanded into a staff of more than 90 experts, gay and straight. Its national headquarters is in New York City, with satellite offices in Atlanta, GA, Chicago, IL, Dallas, TX, Los Angeles, CA, and Washington, DC. Its mission statement reads: "Lambda Legal is a national organization committed to achieving full recognition of the civil rights of lesbians, gay men, bisexuals, transgender people and everyone living with HIV through impact litigation, education and public policy work."

Besides winning its most important lawsuit, the right to its own existence, Lambda Legal has won several high profile cases that have forever changed the course of American history. Among the more significant cases are:

- ***Romer v. Evans*** – In 1996 the Supreme Court ruled by a vote of 6-3 that LBGTQ individuals have the same constitutionally protected rights as any other citizen.

- ***Brandon v. Richardson County*** – In one of its most highly publicized victories, Lambda Legal appealed the case of Brandon Teena, a transgender woman living as a man, who was brutally raped, and later killed. The Sherriff's department not only provided Teena no protection, but also notified the rapists that Teena had pressed charges against them. Their negligence resulted in his murder. After Teena's mother sued and lost, Lambda Legal took up the case. They appealed to the Nebraska Supreme Court which found in their favor stating that the sheriff's abuse of Teena during the rape investigation was "extreme and outrageous, beyond all possible bounds of decency, and is to be regarded as atrocious and utterly intolerable in a civilized community."
  This case was the basis for the critically acclaimed movie *Boys Don't Cry* for which Hillary Swank won the Academy Award for Best Actress in 2000.
- ***Lawrence v. Texas*** – In 2003 the Supreme Court ruled, 6-3, that sodomy between consenting adults in private was constitutionally protected. At the time this new ruling was considered as the most important legal victory for LBGTQ rights.
- ***Obergefell v. Hodges*** – In 2015, Lambda Legal was co-counsel when the Supreme Court, in a 5-4 decision, held that same sex marriages would be recognized as legal, overruling its own prior decision. In a previous precedent setting case, *Varnum v. Brien*, Lambda Legal won a unanimous

decision making Iowa the first state to recognize marriage equality.

Lambda Legal has been involved in other historic cases but it considers the 2003 win striking down sodomy laws and the 2015 marriage equality ruling as its two most important victories granting equal dignity to all LBGTQ individuals.

Lambda Legal is presently involved in numerous lawsuits. Among them are *Karnoski v. Trump*, attempting to lift the ban on transgender individuals in the military; *Harrison v. Mattis*, which challenges the military's policy preventing enlistment, deployment, or commissioning as an officer any person living with HIV; and *Marouf v. Azar* concerning the denial of gay couples to serve as foster parents because they did not "mirror the Holy Family."

Over the years, Fire Island Pines and Cherry Grove have offered refuge in an unfriendly world unwilling to accept gay proclivities. After decades of struggle that resulted in victories as well as defeats, Fire Island still provides that safe haven while facing a future of new challenges, not the least of which are Supreme Court nominations.

Lambda Legal has been hosting fund raisers in the Pines for forty years, the longest, continuous LBGTQ fund raiser in the country. Todd Sears who has hosted "Lambda Legal in the Pines" for years continues to do so. In 2015 Todd instituted the "Pines 20" in an effort to raise $5000 dollars each from 20 individuals or couples. He now intends to call the group the "Pines 78" in recognition of the year of Lambda Legal's first fund raiser. He has been extremely successful, raising hundreds of thousands of dollars over the years.

LAMBDA LEGAL IN WASHINGTON, D.C.
Courtesy of Lambda Legal

Going forward Lambda Legal sees protecting the rights of immigrants, Muslims, people of color and the LBGTQ community as their biggest challenge and it does so not in fear but in solidarity with those communities.

The recent retirement of Justice Anthony Kennedy from the Supreme Court adds to the importance of its efforts. Justice Kennedy was the swing vote in the 5-4 ruling legalizing same sex marriages. Here is his written opinion: "No union is more profound than marriage, for it embodies the highest ideals of love, fidelity, devotion, sacrifice, and family. In forming a marital union, two people become something greater than once they were. As some of the petitioners in these cases demonstrate, marriage embodies a love that may endure even past death. It would misunderstand these men and women to say they disrespect the idea of marriage. Their plea is that they do respect it, respect it so deeply that they seek to find its fulfillment for themselves. Their hope is not to be condemned to live in loneliness, excluded from one of civilization's oldest institutions. They ask for equal dignity in the eyes of the law. The Constitution grants them that right."

Equal dignity for the LBGTQ community is Lambda Legal's raison d'être.

FIRE ISLAND ON THE SMALL SCREEN

Fire Island has had its share of exposure on the big screen (movies), not often but enough to be notable. However, it is not much seen on the small screen (TV) until fairly recently when some cinematographers decided to use Fire Island for its beauty and exotic allure, drawn by its close proximity to NYC.

To touch on just a few movies the earliest may have been the 1926 "The Son of the Shiek" starring Rudolf Valentino and Vilma Banky shot on Fire Island across from Mastic.

Perhaps the most significant was "Last Summer," a coming of age story about burgeoning adolescent sexuality. The renown team of Frank and Eleanor Perry (director and screenwriter respectively), coming off their Academy Award nominations for the highly acclaimed "David and Lisa," choose Ocean Beach and Seaview as the setting for their film. The outstanding cast included Catherine Burns who received an Academy Award nomination for best supporting actress. Other heavyweights included Barbara Hersey, Richard Thomas, and Bruce Davison. Maguire's Restaurant served as headquarters for the film crew.

In 1989, Fire Island played host to the movie "Longtime Companion" again starring Bruce Davison for which he received a nomination as Best Actor in a Supporting Role only to lose out to Joe Pesci in "Goodfellas."

Other movies filmed here include 2008's "What Happens in Vegas," starring Cameron Diaz and Ashton Kutcher, the 2013 HBO movie "The Normal Heart," starring Mark Ruffalo and Joe Mantello, a movie yes, but made for home cinema—the smaller screen.

But as for Fire Island on TV, besides numerous casual mentions the island gets on the evening news and shows such as "Law and Order," and "NYPD Blue," Fire Island had been mostly absent. We did get a plug on "Darts of BBC America" when a young woman said she had learned to play darts barefoot on Fire Island, but mentions like that count as little as a Trump exaggeration.

However with the advent of reality TV, producers have found our island. Back in 1999, Stephen Fry produced the documentary mini-series for Bravo TV entitled "Fire Island". It followed "the real lives and loves of two summer-share household's one gay male, the other lesbian." The show only lasted four episodes.

In 2006, ABC and CTV premiered "One Ocean View," a reality show about eleven twenty-something single New Yorkers (four men and seven women) looking for sex and romance (or both) on weekends at an oceanfront beach house in Corneille Estates. It rated as ABC's least watched show and was cancelled after only two episodes. Its demise was wildly celebrated by Fire Island locals who objected to the presence and behavior of the cast and crew.

The crew, with their long hair and tattoos, was apparently more appealing than the "Ken & Barbie" headliners. Some group-rental babes made inquiries about those hot crew guys at the best source for all good scuttlebutt—the Fire Island News offices. Later that evening those same gals, all gussied up, visited the crew sporting bottles of wine and smug smiles. The show may not have been a hit but the crew sure was.

PEPPERMINT (DRAG QUEEN) FROM TV SHOW "FIRE ISLAND
User:Tenebrae, CC BY-SA 4.0

More recently (Spring of 2017) saw the reprise of another show also titled "Fire Island." It was produced by Kelly Ripa and her husband Mark Consuelos. Mark commented, "We fell in love with Fire Island years ago the minute we stepped off the ferry. We're excited to share the long-standing magic of the island with this new series and to be working again with our Logo family."

This "Fire Island" was about six gay men sharing a super-luxurious oceanfront home in Fire Island Pines, searching for the "romance, temptation and thrills that have brought the LGBTQ community to the island for decades."

Even before the new season began, however, *The Advocate*, the largest LBGTQ publication in the U.S., published an article decrying the behavior exhibited on the show as detrimental to the reputation of the gay community as a whole. The gay community "must choose to elevate public perception of us as best we can. We are above this..." read the article. Whether or not that piece had any bearing on the success or failure of the show will remain unanswered. It ran for only seven episodes.

TRAVEL CHANNEL'S "HOTEL IMPOSSIBLE" CREW.
OCEAN BEACH 2016
(Photo by Shoshanna McCollum)

The Fire Island Pines, given its cachet, and diverse, albeit upper class gay and straight community, has proven to be a prime location. Captain David J. Mahler, President of TCS Marine Services, docks his boat in the Pines for the season and has provided transportation for several reality stars.

Captain David had a top secret 1 a.m. mission to ferry Cher from Sayville to the Pines for a Hillary Clinton fundraiser. When Cher arrived the town went wild, cranking up her music for all to hear.

Captain Dave also transported three stranded "Fire Island" cast members, and their dog, to the Pines. While docked at the Blue Whale restaurant he was within a "short Grey Poupon bottle toss" from his yacht to friends who had appeared on "Below Decks." The contingent of the "Real Housewives of NY" in the Pines made a mockery of themselves. They were obnoxious, arrogant and nasty, followed everywhere by their idiotic fawning fans.

Otherwise, there are, of course, documentaries and short movies: "Greetings from Fire Island" may be the best travelogue; "Baymen" filmed on Fire Island and the Great South Bay; "Blinded," shot in Ocean Beach; "Modern Tide: Midcentury Architecture on Long Island," Fire Island Pines; "Andrew Geller: A Spacial [sic] Encounter," Ocean Bay Park; "The Irish Whiskey Rebellion," shot mostly in Saltaire, Long Cove and Skunk Hollow where a cottage was set afire. The list goes on.

One odd-ball 2018 entry is the quirky, crowd-funded, "The Perfect Martini-O," a comedic look at two guys' search for the perfect martini in off-season Ocean Beach.

But no matter how artists try to portray Fire Island, cool or crazy, drunk or sober, gay or straight, the island remains a Lady—stately and beautiful, wild as a hurricane, and as self-possessed as mythic shadows dancing in sunken forests. No one can possess her though many try, tattooing her with their own impermanent imaginings. Come visit the Lady. Stay a while and enjoy her charms, but one day you too will have to leave her. She will remain, welcoming new lovers who wait to claim her. She is not fickle. She will love them like she loved you—loved you like no other—

yet—just like all the others. So, treasure the Lady and she will share her treasures with you for a moment—maybe more than a moment if you're lucky.

A BRIEF HISTORY OF PANDEMICS
AND FIRE ISLAND

As isolated as Fire Island is it has had more than its share of pandemics. COVID-19 is only the latest, and thanks to the leadership of mayors, police officers, business owners and just plain folk, Fire Island has skirted most of the damage inflicted on the rest of the world. Actual cases of the disease on the island are few with no reported deaths, but damage to the commercial sectors was severe. Most retail stores were able to open and restaurants provided outdoor dining with some limited indoor dining as well. Masks were required and social distancing encouraged as much as possible in the crowded communities.

THE FIJI'S OF FIRE ISLAND

The first documented pandemic on Fire Island was one not of its own making. Early September 1892, the steamship *Normannia* from Hamburg, Germany, arrived off New York with five passengers sick with cholera, and with another four already dead. Cholera, caused by bacteria, is a particularly deadly infectious disease with a mortality rate approaching 70 percent. To protect the public, the ship was ordered to quarantine in lower New York harbor.

Then, to ensure the health of the remaining 600 or so passengers who showed no signs of illness, it was decided to transfer them to a sanctuary ashore. In a quick, secret, closed-door meeting, New York's Governor Roswell P. Flower purchased the Surf Hotel, located near

Democrat Point, Fire Island, as the location for quarantining the passengers.

However, the proceedings of that secret meeting were leaked to the public and the shellfish, fishing, and charter boat industries in the Great South Bay area took an immediate economic hit as existing commercial contracts were cancelled. A purported 5,000 to 6,000 jobs from Babylon to Patchogue were in jeopardy.

Islip Town officials filed an injunction to prevent the ship from landing at the Surf Hotel on Fire Island, and ordered 20 armed constables to enforce the injunction, but the following day the NYS Supreme Court vacated that injunction.

Meanwhile, some passengers on the *Normannia* had been transferred to a smaller vessel, the *Cepheus*, with directions to land them at the hotel's dock. Some baymen attempted to burn down the Surf Hotel and when the *Cepheus* arrived the following day it was met by an angry mob. The heavily-armed crowd of 300-400 refused to let the ship dock.

HARPER'S WEEKLY ARTIST DEPICTION OF THE MOB
MEETING THE "CEPHUS" TO PREVENT PASSENGERS FROM
DISEMBARKING AT THE SURF HOTEL 1892

In response Gov. Flower called out the 13th and 69th
Army regiments as well as some naval reserves to quell the
rebellion and facilitate the landing of the desperate
passengers. After several days of skirmishes, the
government forces were able to ensconce the passengers
safely in the hotel. After three weeks of quarantine, with no
new cases of cholera developing, the anticipated epidemic
never materialized and the passengers were released to
return to their normal, everyday lives.

In the Oct. 1, 1892, edition of *Illustrated American*,
an article, entitled "The Fijis of Fire Island" reported the
incident as follows: "Panic took possession of the
inhabitants of Islip, Bay Shore, and Babylon and drove

them insane temporarily. That is the best excuse that can be made for their heartless, brutal cruelty... [T]hey were ignorant savages. Such acts as theirs are committed by barbarians in China and the South Seas...Their behavior was a disgrace not only to American manhood, but to civilization."

CAMP CHEERFUL

The next pandemic that landed on Fire Island shores occurred in 1926, amid an outbreak of poliomyelitis. In response, the New York Rotary Club established, funded and ran a camp for children threatened by polio. They called it "Camp Cheerful." Each year more than 300 youngsters from NYC were cared for. Every two and half weeks a new group would arrive to take advantage of Fire Island's fresh air, salt water and sandy beaches with hopes of helping to heal the afflicted.

The camp consisted of a row of bungalows for the children, a mess hall, shop, a recreation hall, kitchen, administration building, and quarters for the hired help.

Unfortunately, after only 12 years of operation the camp was destroyed by the hurricane of 1938 and was never rebuilt.

That was not the end of interest in Fire Island, however. Oral history accounts from Fire Island in the early twentieth century indicate that families in New York City area increasingly sought refuge from the threat of polio outbreaks during the hot summer months, contributing to the emerging popularity of Fire Island communities. The trend continued long after medical researcher Jonas Salk developed a vaccine in 1955.

HIV/AIDS

But no pandemic devastated Fire Island more than the HIV/AIDS epidemic that decimated the gay populations of Cherry Grove and the Fire Island Pines.

In the late 1970s, the Stonewall riots were already a decade old. The LBGTQ community was filled with pride, their lifestyles slowly gaining more public acceptance. Gay couples could hold hands in public. The Grove and the Pines seemed like paradise. There was disco dancing, costumed carousing, a tea party every afternoon, and a pool party every night—all night. The photographer Meryl Meisler described the gaiety of it all. "Cherry Grove, the Pines, and all of Fire Island was a magical place. One day, thousands and thousands of Monarch Butterflies descended and were there for the entire day. It was really magical." Life there, she said, was "absolutely stunning."

Then the party ended like the curtain coming down mid-show. In 1980 one of the first cases in the U.S. of a new deadly disease occurred in the Pines when all the gay men sharing a house came down with this mysterious disease and died within weeks of each other. The disease was unknown and nameless.

It was initially nicknamed the "Saint Disease," after a lower East Side disco where patrons were free to explore the heights of hedonism, sex with whomever, whenever, and drugs without drugstores, only to return home with a sickness without a name that killed them.

Friends started dying. One weekend they were out on the dance floor, the next week there was a for-sale sign in their front yard. If you called and learned that a phone had been disconnected you did not wonder why. It was a plague that no one wanted to talk about.

LOCATION OF "THE SAINT" ONCE THE "VATICAN OF DISCO," LATER THE FILLMORE EAST, NOW A BANK
Public Domain

In 1981, the New York Times published the first article that detailed the extent of the epidemic, pointing to gay sex as the method of transmission. The reality of the situation could no longer be ignored. A "gay cancer" had come for a visit with no signs of leaving.

The Centers for Disease Control recognized a disease pattern that was killing gay men in LA and NY and called it AIDS, an acronym for Acquired Immune Deficiency Syndrome. AIDS itself does not kill, but a weakened immune system allows infectious diseases to attack the body, usually with deadly consequences.

Scientists in both the U.S. and Europe were searching for the causes of the disease and in 1985 jointly discovered the virus responsible. They named it the Human Immunodeficiency Virus (HIV). Research continued, doctors now searching for cures. First there was AZT, then the HAART cocktail of pills and finally in 1997, a pill that prevented infections in 90 percent of gay men became available.

However it was not just a pill that saved Fire Island's male gay communities. The lesbian sisterhood stepped up and assumed more leadership roles. They lived alongside the men who were dying, marched with them refusing to allow policy makers to marginalize the horrific disease. Compassion and inclusivity is what made the once ravaged Fire Island communities more resilient than ever. Today the Cherry Grove fire department is predominantly female, including its first ever fire chief. AIDS is still with us, but the horrific pandemic is over.

CHERRY GROVE FIRE DEPARTMENT
Courtesy of Cherry Grove Archives Collection

A new pandemic, COVID-19, haunts us and some things will never be the same. But life goes on. Celebrate by doing the right thing—wear your mask, maintain social distancing, wash your hands often and get vaccinated.

Remember, history is watching.

Fire Island News Editor Shoshanna McCollum also contributed to this article.

FIRE ISLAND NATIONAL SEASHORE A WORLD HERITAGE SITE?

WORLD HERITAGE SITES (WHS) are places listed by the United Nations Educational, Scientific and Cultural Organization (UNESCO) as being of special cultural and/or physical significance. Once a World Heritage Site designation has been assigned, world-class expertise is brought to bear to protect that area. There are 1,031 sites (and counting) throughout the world, 24 of which were added in 2015 including the San Antonio Missions in Texas. The Statue of Liberty is a WHS, as are the Great Barrier Reef in Australia, Easter Island (Rapa Nui), Petra in Jordan, Machu Picchu, and the Great Wall of China.

NPS/FIRE IsLAND NATIONAL SEASHORE
Courtesy of NPS

To become listed, the site must be of "universal value and meet at least one out of 10 selection criteria." These criteria seek to protect and preserve the sites, linking the concepts of conservation with the preservation of cultural properties while recognizing the need to balance those concerns with the ways in which people interact with the sites.

Fire Island meets at least three criteria as specified by UNESCO:

Criteria V – "to be an outstanding example of a traditional human settlement, land-use which is representative of a culture (cultures), or human interaction with the environment especially when it has become vulnerable under the impact of irreversible change."

Fire Island is a barrier island, 32 miles long by approximately 1⁄2 mile wide. Twenty-six of those miles are administered by the National Park Service (NPS) as authorized by Congress with the creation of the Fire Island National Seashore (FINS) in 1964. The Fire Island National Seashore extends 1,000 feet into the Atlantic Ocean, its southern boundary, and 4,000 feet into the Great South Bay, Patchogue Bay, Bellport Bay, Narrow Bay and Moriches Bay, its northern boundaries. It also contains a number of small islands, sand flats and wetlands, along with the William Floyd Estate in Mastic Beach.

Barrier beaches such as Fire Island provide indispensable protection for the mainland from flooding and erosion, and afford shelter from periodic hurricanes. As reported by the Fire Island National Seashore Short-term Community Storm Surge Protection Plan, Environmental Assessment: "Barrier islands such as Fire Island provide unique ocean- side habitat and protection from the flooding and erosion of the mainland shorelines.

Criteria VII – "to contain superlative natural phenomena or areas of exceptional beauty and aesthetic importance."

Fire Island is home to Sunken Forest, a national treasure, a very rare ecological commodity, and one of only two known locations on Atlantic barrier islands: the Sunken Forest, part of Fire Island National Seashore, New York, and the Sandy Hook holly forest, part of Gateway National Recreation Area, New Jersey.

STAND OF ENDANGERED HOLLY TREES.-.SUNKEN
FOREST – FIRE ISLAND NATIONAL SEASHORE
nps.gov

Sunken Forest has a global rarity rank, meaning: "Critically Imperiled or Imperiled globally – At very high or high risk of extinction due to rarity or other factors; typically 20 or fewer populations or locations in the world, very few individuals, very restricted range, few remaining acres (or miles of stream), and/or steep declines."

In addition, Fire Island Lighthouse is an historic and important aid to navigation. It was the first sighting of America for passengers on transatlantic ships arriving from

Europe during the 19th and 20th centuries. Today the lighthouse is a beacon that attracts 125,000 visitors a year.

The Otis Pike Wilderness Area on the eastern reaches of Fire Island occupies eight miles of virtually pristine beaches, high dunes covered in wildflowers, and seaside artifacts. It is the only Wilderness Area in New York State.

The William Floyd Estate, also a part of FINS, a 613-acre property located in Mastic Beach, was added to FINS in 1965. It once belonged to William Floyd, a signer of the Declaration of Independence.

Criteria X – "to contain the most important and significant natural habitats for in-situ conservation of biological diversity, including those threatened species of outstanding universal value from the point of view of science or conservation."

Fire Island is the habitat for several endangered species. The Piping Plover (*Charadrius melodus*) has been reduced to a population of only 6,500 and Fire Island is one its last remaining breeding areas. The Roseate Tern (*Sterna dougallii*), also a resident species, is federally and state endangered, as is the Least Tern (*Sternula antitarum*).

The Seabeach Amaranth (*Amaranthus pumilius)*, a federally threatened annual plant species, grows on Fire Island beaches. The Seabeach Knotweed (*Polygonum glaucum*) is another rare plant that makes Fire Island its home.

Three species of endangered whales ply the waters of the Atlantic Ocean off Fire Island. They are the Humpback Whale (*Megaptera* novaeangliae), the Fin Whale (*Balaenoptera physalus*), and the Northern Right

Whale (*Eubalaena glacialis*). Five federally endangered species of sea turtles have been documented on Fire Island although none nest there: Kemp's Ridley Turtle (*Lepidochelys kempii*), the Leatherback Turtle (*Dermochelys* coriacea), and the Hawksbill Turtle (*Eretmochelys imbricata*) are federally endangered species, while the Loggerhead Turtle (*Caretta caretta*) and Green Turtle (*Chelonia mydas*) are federally threatened.

There is a need for world-class expertise to preserve the natural treasures of the seashore and the barrier beach island. Addressing imminent threats to the planet because of climate change and rising sea levels will require the expertise obtainable through designation as a World Heritage Site. To this end, Jerry Stoddard and Irving Like formed the Fire Island Conservancy, a 501(c) (3) not-for-profit corporation to advance the long-term protection of the barrier island and its communities, and to gain World Heritage Site status for FINS.

Irving Like, Esq., one of the founding members of the Citizens Committee for the Fire Island National Seashore, was, in part, responsible for the defeat of the Robert Moses highway.

Jerry Stoddard, president of the Fire Island Association from 1987 to 2011, was a bit more circumspect. "Fire Island is unique. Those who live here celebrate that. At the same time that they want to protect that fact, they want to preserve their uniqueness... It is important to remember that each individual is different. Some are interested in the commercial aspect, some want solitude. There should be a system under UNESCO, where all can be formally recognized and accepted. There is room for all."

There are, however, other well-argued points of view in opposition to the idea. The one most often voiced, is the question of sovereignty. Will the UN, through UNESCO, control and/or manage FINS, and...what about the law of unintended consequences? Some members of Congress argue that such a designation infringes on the national sovereignty of the U.S., allowing foreigners to determine how we use our lands and natural resources. Some also maintain that Congress does not have enough of an influence on which U.S. sites are nominated to the World Heritage List. Presently, the executive branch of the government can make an assessment as to what will create pollution problems, traffic tie-ups, the burdening of municipal services, and price inflation. And, of course, political shenanigans can never be discounted.

Indeed, tourism is a two-edged sword. It is one of the world's largest industries. The World Travel and Tourism Council estimates that tourism generates 12 percent of the world's total GNP. Visitor fees, concessions, and donations provide funds needed for restoration and protection efforts. The answer to this dichotomy is the implementation of responsible and sustainable tourism policies.

UNESCO recognizes that management and sovereignty remain with the country where the site is located "without prejudice to property rights provided by national legislation."

UNESCO can only monitor and evaluate these sites, offering technical advice and assistance. In fact, the convention emphasizes that the countries in which these sites are located are themselves responsible for protecting and conserving those sites.

The worst that UNESCO can do is to remove a site's designation. This has happened only twice, once in Oman's Arabian Oryx Sanctuary because of poaching and habitat degradation, and the other in Germany's Dresden Elbe Valley because of the construction of a bridge that bisected the site.

The former example illustrates the continuing danger of species extinction (one of WHS cornerstone concerns) and the latter highlights the fact that UNESCO does, in fact, have no power over local governments.

Pope Francis' Encyclical *Laudato Si'*, which addressed climate change directly, engenders hope for support on an international scale.

Fire Island serves a population in excess of 12 million people within a 50-mile radius. This area includes the Statue of Liberty (a World Heritage Site itself), New York City with all its financial, cultural, and artistic treasures, and the United Nations headquarters, home of UNESCO.

Among WHS supporters is State Senator Thomas Croci who states, "This nation has many treasures, but the Fire Island National Seashore is of such a distinct character, it is unequivocally worthy of such designation."

The previous articles were all published in the Fire Island News The following three were not, but I consider them important, or interesting enough, to be included.

HOW MANY FIRE ISLANDS ARE THERE ON OUR PLANET?

So far, there are 17 locations named Fire Island on the globe, thirteen in America, three in Canada and one in Russia.

Here they are.

Just as there is confusion about the origin of the name of our Fire Island, little is known about how these other islands got their names, but where that information is available it is included in the following descriptions.

New York - Fire Island, Suffolk County – Our own slice of paradise, 5 miles off the south shore of Long Island. Just to the north of Fire Island are two smaller islands. We pass them when the ferry from Bay Shore takes its western route to the island.

NEW YORK - EAST FIRE ISLAND – Also known as Hollins Island is uninhabited with no ferry service and is accessible only by boat.

The island was originally purchased from Winnequaheagh, Sachem of Connetquot back in 1687. Harry Bowly "H.B." Hollins, an American railroad magnate purchased the island in 1906 as the site for a grand estate, but H.B. went bankrupt in 1913 and the dream went unrealized.

Rumors exist that Captain Kidd's treasure from the Spanish Main is buried on this island. Consequently, it is sometimes referred to as Money Island and has been the destination of many treasure hunters.

Public Domain

NEW YORK - WEST FIRE ISLAND – A smaller island with five homes and no electric service. Three houses from West Island were floated across the bay to Ocean Beach, Fire Island in 1970 and presently sit just to the west of Maguire's Bay Front Restaurant.

MONTANA - FIRE ISLAND, (FLATHEAD COUNTY) – This is a 13 acre island with a four-site campground in the Hungry Horse Reservoir accessible only by boat. It is about 25 miles SE of Whitefish, Montana and 55 miles south of the Canadian border. The Hungry Horse area got its name from two freight horses who wandered away in the severe winter of 1900/01. For a month they struggled in the deep snow and nearly starved to death but were nursed back to health. The Hungry Horse name stuck.

MONTANA - FIRE ISLAND, (SWEET GRASS COUNTY) – A small island in south-central Montana at a bend in the Boulder River, a tributary of the Yellowstone River, about one mile south of Big Timber and 50 miles east of Bozeman, Montana. The Boulder River Valley was used in filming *A River Runs Through It* and *The Horse Whisperer*.

MINNESOTA - FIRE ISLAND – A two acre uninhabited island in Snowbank Lake, Minnesota, located approximately 100 miles NNE of Duluth.

MICHIGAN - FIRE ISLAND, DRUMMOND TOWNSHIP – A small inhabited island with half a dozen structures located in Potagannissing Bay, Lake Huron, approximately one-half mile off Harbor Island National Wildlife Refuge, 50 miles east of Mackinac Island.

MICHIGAN - FIRE ISLAND, ISLE ROYALE – An isolated two acre island located in Tobin Harbor, Isle Royal National Park. The park, designated a National Wilderness Area, is a remote island cluster in Lake Superior.

LOUISIANA - FIRE ISLAND, VERMILLION PARISH – Vermillion Parish is located midway between New Orleans, Louisiana and Houston, Texas. It has numerous so-called islands that are really marshes. They are sometimes surrounded by man-made ditches and canals. Many have road access. According to the local Sheriffs office, Fire Island was named because the area once caught fire and the name stuck. It has an elevation of only 3 feet.

ALASKA - FIRE ISLAND, ALEUTIAN ISLANDS – This is a 5 acre island in the eastern Aleutians near Bogoslof Island in the frigid Bering Sea. It is cold, remote, inhospitable and has no anchorages. President Teddy Roosevelt made Bogoslof and New Bogoslof (Fire Island) bird sanctuaries. Both are active volcanic islands, but Fire Island is the newer of the two giving rise to its name.

ALASKA - FIRE ISLAND, KASHEVAROF PASSAGE – This is another isolated, uninhabited island. It is one-half mile long by one-quarter mile wide in the Kashevarof Passage off the NE coast of Prince of Wales Island.

ALASKA - FIRE ISLAND, COOK INLET, ANCHORAGE – This is the largest and most well known of all the Fire Islands save our own. It is almost seven square miles in size, a mere three miles off the coast of Anchorage with insufficient fresh water resources and no permanent residents as per the 2000 census.

It has gone through several name changes. Originally it was called Nutul'Iy (Object that Stands in the Water in the *Dena'ina* language of the Alaskan natives.)

British naval Captain James Cook's men named it Currant Island and in 1794 Captain George Vancouver called it Turnagain Island.

Shem Pete, a renowned elder of the Dena'ina Indians, in the book *Shem Pete's Alaska: The Territory of the Upper Cook Inlet Dena'ina*, gave this account of how the island got its name. "Captain Cook came ashore and built a fire there at Fire Island ... and they ate there ... In order for them to light that fire on it, he named Fire Island, 'that which is burning on it.'" In 1895 the U.S. Coast and Geodetic Survey made the name official.

A Dena'ina village once existed on the island and fish camps thrived there until 1970. It was a U.S. Army observation station during WWII and in 1951 the Air Force established an air defense radar station there equipped with Nike surface to air missiles. Some resourceful Air Force personnel created the "Breakneck Hill" in the Alaska Lost Ski Project on the island complete with an 800 foot tow lift area during this era. The devastating 1964 Alaska earthquake collapsed the airfield into the ocean. The AF base was closed in 1969 and the Cook Inlet Region, Inc (CIRI) corporation took ownership of the 90% if the island in 1982. It began building a wind farm on the island in 2009 and by 2012 it was up and running.

WIND FARM, FIRE ISLAND, ALASKA
Courtesy of Fire Island Wind, LLC, Ciri.com

Currently, the island houses an 11 turbine, 17.6 megawatt wind farm operated by Fire Island Wind, LLC, a subsidiary of CIRI. The towers are 260 feet high and are connected to the Anchorage power grid via an underwater transmission line. It has the capacity of powering 7000 Anchorage homes with its current configuration, but the project has been approved for a total of 33 turbines which can increase its electrical capacity to 52.8 MW.

There is an annual Fire Island Walk in July from Kincaid Beach, Anchorage across mud flats to Fire Island and back. Kincaid Park is Anchorage's only sandy beach with tall bluffs on one side and spectacular views of Cook Inlet and Fire Island on the other.

This walk (barefoot is recommended because shoes get lost in the mud and "it feels good on the feet") is approximately 3 to 4 hours there and back and is only for the brave. Silt collects at the head of Cook Inlet, just off Anchorage creating these flats. The surface, when the tide is out, varies from hard packed to gooey, gooey enough to trap people and hold them captive as the tide comes in to slowly drown them. The tide range is 25 feet and comes in at the rate of one inch per minute. As one scientist noted, "The average person from ground to nose is only one hour tall." Rescues by the Anchorage Fire Department have become common.

ALASKA - FIRE ISLAND, NENANA RIVER, DENALI – This is the newest Fire Island. A small island on the Nenana River adjacent to the Denali Park Chalet Resort has become known lately as Fire Island because of its similarity in shape to Anchorage's Fire Island and because of the fires built there by the resort employees. Can newer Fire Islands be far behind?

CANADA - FIRE ISLAND, SIOUX NARROWS NESTOR FALLS, ONTARIO – A 60 acre island in Lake of the Woods, one of the world's largest freshwater lakes with 14,000 islands and 65,000 miles of shoreline. It is near Sioux Narrows and Nestor Falls, 140 miles E of Winnipeg.

CANADA - FIRE ISLAND, FRENCH RIVER, ONTARIO – A tiny half-acre island on the French River, 300 miles W of Montreal.

CANADA - FIRE ISLAND, QUEEN CHARLOTTE STRAIT, BRITISH COLUMBIA – A 45 acre island in the Queen Charlotte Strait, 10 miles off the coast of Vancouver Island, 210 miles NW of Victoria, BC.

RUSSIA - FIRE ISLAND, OGNENNY OSTROV

Volgodskiy Pyatak, or simply Pyatak, houses one of the most brutal prisons on Earth. Located 300 miles N of Moscow on Lake Beloye (White Lake), the prison was originally built as a Russian Orthodox monastery in 1571 by St Cyril who saw "a column of fire" hit the island. It is also called "Fiery Island."

After 1917 it became a prison for "enemies of the revolution," and then, under Stalin, a penal colony, and finally after his death a maximum security prison holding mostly serial killers.

VOLGODSKIY PYATAK
wikimedia.org

Like Alcatraz, Petak, as it is called by guards and prisoners alike, is surrounded by water. There are only two approaches to the prison. One is by foot over two rickety wooden bridges. The other is by prison boat. No one has ever escaped.

Prisoners are kept in small, two-man cells for 22.5 hours a day. The remaining time they exercise in a small cage outside. A single rule violation can result in six month of solitary confinement in small, dark cells with a fold-down bed and a metal bucket. No books are permitted. There are no lavatories, or proper washing facilities which accounts for the high rate of tuberculosis at the prison. When inmates die, their bodies are buried in a nearby graveyard with one or two guards present. No relatives or inmates can attend. A western journalist remarked, "In a country where brutality and hopelessness are common currency, Petak is as bad as it gets."

Meanwhile, the prison sits on one of the most beautiful lakes in all of Russia. White Lake is a 450 square mile lake almost circular in shape. It is surrounded by stone churches, ancient monasteries, the Venus Pavilion in Gatchina Palace Park, picturesque villages, and forests reflected in its blue waters, none of which the prisoners can appreciate.

So...

So, as you sit in the sun reading this with by the gently chop of the Great South Bay on one side and the white crested waves of the Atlantic Ocean thundering on the other, take a moment (or two) to reflect how truly blessed we are with this Fire Island—the best Fire Island on the globe.

THE POLITICAL CUDGEL OF RACISM

Lord knows Fire Islanders have every reason to hate Robert Moses for his attempts to jam a four-lane highway down the center of Fire Island against the popular will, but, perhaps, dislike would be a more judicious choice of word than hate.

Hate is a four letter word. The airwaves are clogged with hate these days, smothering reason. Hate hides any number of egregious evils beneath the shade of its wide, black umbrella. Racism is one.

Robert Moses has been accused of racism, but is it true?

His accomplishments are legendary, too many to list here, but some of the more notable are the development of Lincoln Center, the UN complex, Jones Beach, the building of at least five bridges, six expressways, and hundreds of miles of tree-lined parkways. Under the rationale of "slum clearance" he was also responsible for five middle-income housing developments. Yet, in spite of all these achievements, or perhaps because of them, the man is accused of bigotry.

Charges of racism in politics are nothing new. Xenophobia, distrust of anyone different, has roots at least as far back as ancient Greece and Rome. The Greeks coined the word "barbarian" meaning those not members of Greek states, but racism extends beyond just a distrust of "others." Racism sees groups of others as inferior, and

269

nowadays that inferiority has often been attached to skin color. Lately the news has been filled with charges of racism, true or not, exaggerated or not, accusations used as cudgels to silence opposition. The cudgel of racism is an equal-opportunity weapon for politicians on both the Left and the Right.

So was it politics or was Robert Moses a racist? Given his myriad accomplishments a careful examination of the charges seems in order.

There are several charges. Most come from the seminal, 1300 page, Pulitzer Prize winning biography called "Power Broker: Robert Moses and the Fall of New York" by Robert A. Caro. In it Caro describes Moses as "the most racist human being I had ever really encountered."

Caro's most damning charge is that Moses purposely built the bridges along the parkway approaches to Jones Beach so low that buses transporting "undesireables" would be unable to pass beneath. When Moses was reminded that buses were already prohibited from NY parkways, Sid Shapiro, Moses' chief aide, quoted Moses as replying, "Legislation can always be changed. It's very hard to tear down a bridge once it's up." Karl Grossman, an esteemed colleague who knew Shapiro, vouches for the authenticity of this quote.

There is, however, an argument refuting this interpretation, one corroborated by history. Moses hired Gilmore D. Clarke as a consultant. He followed Clarke's early designs for his parkways to Jones Beach., including their bridges. Clarke had built his parkways in Westchester

270

County, and Clarke's bridges, it turns out, were also too low for buses.

Another accusation concerns Moses' construction of NYC swimming pools. He is charged with ordering the water temperature of the pools to be kept "deliberately icy" because he had heard that black people would not swim in cold water.

To date there is no proof of this accusation and it continues to be challenged. In fact, during the summer of 1936 Moses opened 11 outdoor pools across NYC. They were so impressive in both design and technological advancement that they were recognized by the Landmarks Preservation Commission. One of the 11 pools (originally the Colonial Park Pool—now called the Jackie Robinson Pool) is in Harlem and is considered one of the best public works of the New Deal. Approximately 25,000 folk attended its opening ceremony. Robert Moses was introduced to loud applause by the famous dancer/actor and civil rights pioneer Bill "Bojangles" Robinson.

Another charge against Moses is his use of racially insensitive motifs on the wrought-iron trellises of the Harlem comfort station in Riverside Park. He had them decorated with monkeys. This part is true.

Karl Grossman published an anecdote citing Moses' racism. This one concerns the 1964/1965 World's Fair in Queens, NY. Grossman went to the World's Fair on opening day to report on protests organized by the Congress of Racial Equality (CORE) on the unfair hiring practices at the Fair. The protestors had no sooner arrived on scene and unfurled their banners before they were set upon by private security forces that proceeded to beat them with clubs, actions so brutal they were akin to the violence then occurring in the deep South. The publication of this story, along with Grossman's photos, incensed Moses. The World's Fair was his baby. He called Grossman's publisher and editor and had Grossman promptly fired.

Among his many titles, Moses was chairman of New York's City's Slum Clearing Commission. As such he replaced "slums" with middle income housing developments seemingly unconcerned about the racial makeup of the neighborhoods he was destroying. Such tactics fueled his reputation as a racist.

Jane Jacobs author of "The Death and Life of Great American Cities" was Moses nemesis. She argued against "slum clearance" highlighting its social and cultural costs, the loss of strong neighborhoods and their unique traditions. Moses' answer: "Those who can, build. Those who can't, criticize."

Even though he was in no way involved, Robert Moses also gets blamed for the Brooklyn Dodgers move to L.A. in 1957, not racist but certainly wildly unpopular.

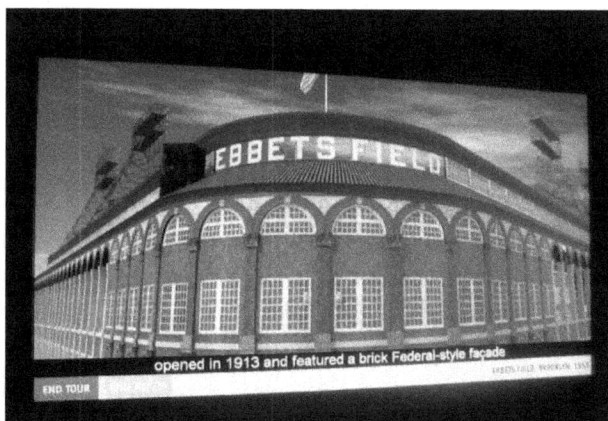

EBBETS FIELD IN ITS GLORY DAYS, WHERE THE BROOKLYN DODGERS PLAYED.
The Glory Days - Ebbets Field video tour" by wallyg CC BY-NC-ND 2.0

There is little question that Moses was arrogant. His arrogance transformed the young idealist into an old man obsessed with the acquisition and application of power. Moses was intransigent in his belief that the future belonged to the automobile. His designs reflect this single-minded, car-culture obsession, and he is widely condemned for it. His critics assert that he cared more about cars than he did about people.

But was Robert Moses a racist?

There are ancient folktales across cultures involving "tar-baby" themes. In his collection of "Uncle Remus" stories, the author, Joel Chandler Harris, tells us a cautionary tale taken from the African-American oral tradition about a tar-baby. The villainous Br'er Fox concocts a plan to punish the trickster Br'er Rabbit for his

273

ongoing misdeeds. Br'er Fox builds a doll made from lumps of tar and dresses it up. Along comes Br'er Rabbit who greets the tar-baby but gets no response. Infuriated by what he perceives as insulting behavior, Br'er Rabbit punches the tar-baby and gets stuck in the tar. The more he struggles to free himself, the more entrapped he becomes.

BRER RABBIT AND THE TAR BABY
"Tar-Baby and Other Rhymes (Frost/Kemble)"
By laurakgibbs is licensed under CC BY-NC-SA 2.0

Racism is like that tar-baby—once engaged, forever besmeared. In the story, Br'er Fox punishes Br'er Rabbit by throwing him into the briar patch, Br'er Rabbit's home, and the culprit escapes any real punishment.

Life is usually not so forgiving.

FIRE ISLAND NEWS – BIRTH OF A NEWSPAPER

FIRE ISLAND NEWS
Fire Island's Longest Running News Source since 1957

The *Fire Island News* has been around since 1957. It may be the adopted child of *The Fire Islander* founded in 1954 by *The New Yorker* theater critic Walcott Gibbs and friends—or not. There is some confusion on this point.

Prior to *The Fire Islander* there was *The Fire Island Reporter*. It was started by Rafael M. Steinberg, and published from July 15, 1949, to September 8, 1951, as a weekly, independent newspaper with stories of general interests to Ocean Beach, Seaview and vicinity. Copies are on file at the Queens Borough Public Library.

Memories being what they are, there are conflicting stories about the origins of *The Fire Islander* and *The Fire Island News*. One story credited to the *Ocean Beach Bicentennial Handbook and Directory 1976*, using Davis Erhardt's personal communication as its source, states that *The Fire Islander,* was published from May 28, 1954, to July 27, 1956. It was started by Ocean Beach residents Bill Birmingham and Herman Wechsler, and essayist and drama critic for *The New Yorker,* Wolcott Gibbs

It quickly developed a sophisticated panache with the help of writers such as James Thurber, Herman Wouk, Fred Allen and John Lardner—among others.

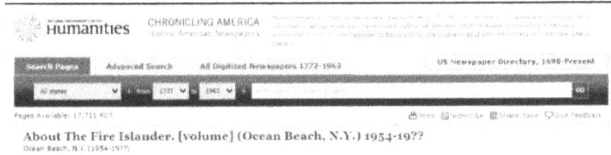

LIBRARY OF CONGRESS
RECORD OF *THE FIRE ISLANDER*

The paper centered its attention on local Fire Island issues such as protection of the dunes, construction of tennis courts, a new yacht basin, and overfishing. When asked why he turned his usually acerbic tongue into such civic minded activities, Wolcott Gibbs replied, "I'm in love with the goddamn beach." With this real concern for the welfare of Fire Island the paper's weekly circulation grew to a respectable 2,500 units. The price was 10 cents a copy.

According to Gibbs, in 1957, his health failing, claims he sold the paper to a group headed by the teenage Jay Garfield Trien—or did he? In Gibbs' farewell he wrote, "We expect to be contributors from time to time, and the paper always will, of course, have our best wishes and first spiritual support ....Beyond that, however, we are as dead as so many dinosaurs. It may be just as well." Gibbs exercised his barbed wit right up to the end.

However, in an article in the Fire Island News printed in 2017, written by journalist Timothy Bolger,

Gibb's story is refuted. Bolger wrote, "There are some published accounts that Trien bought the Fire Islander, a defunct paper founded by Wolcott Gibbs, a critic for The New Yorker who stopped publishing his paper in '56. Trien said he tried to buy the paper, but was rebuffed. The attempted sale, combined with a desire by some to romanticize the News by linking its history to Gibbs, appears to be the source of this falsehood that reverberates to this day." Appreciating Gibbs' caustic crust, Bolger may very well have nailed it.

This newspaper was called *The Fire Island Weekly* for the first two years of its life but was then changed to the *Fire Island News*. It was published out of Trien's Bayberry home in Ocean Beach their first year and they moved the operation five times in five years before settling into a semi-permanent office on Bay Walk, all the while struggling to expand the paper's reach out to the island's eighteen scattered communities.

Within three years the *Fire Island News* was firmly in the black, turning out a polished 16 to 20 page weekly to its 4000 subscribers. The price of the paper had increased to 15 cents (the equivalent of $1.25 in today's money) with a subscription for the whole summer season costing $1.50 back then.

A typical paper from the late fifties, early sixties would be strictly black and white, front page all news, with roughly 30% of the paper taken up by advertisements including classifieds. The vast majority of the ads were from local Fire Island businesses, with less than 10% from NYC organizations. Back then the primary issue was Robert Moses' attempt to put a road down the length of the island and the nefarious methods he was using to do so. The paper was a major influence in spreading the word among the island's many communities about the efforts individuals and groups made to counter, and ultimately defeat, Moses.

Editorials occasionally seem dated and often shifted from one side of the argument to the other like Fire Island summer breezes.

The paper included columns from various communities along the beach, insuring that their local issues and festivities were also covered. As a welcome bonus, it carried the latest Jules Feiffer cartoon each week, an addition that gave the paper a Greenwich Village cred, a sophistication reflective of the island's cosmopolitan swagger.

When Trien went off to study law, he turned the running of the paper over to his mother, Bee Garfield who, besides being the bookkeeper, also wrote the column, "Barefeet 'N Wagons." Bea kept the readers abreast of the up-to-the-minute goings-on, with a little juicy gossip thrown in to make everyone feel right at home. She ran the paper until 1987 when she turned the paper over to Trien's wife, Ilkido, who ran it for another decade.

The *Fire Island News* was run successfully by the Trien family for forty years. By 1996 the pass-along readership had increased to 35,000 with issues ranging in length from 45 to 85 pages. The paper was purchased by Nicole Pressley Wolf, in what she described as, "The momentary insanity of youth!"

The widespread use of the internet has caused chaos in the newspaper industry and Fire Island was not immune.

The Fire Island News went through a lengthy period of loss of readership and incompetent management and was almost lost to history before being rescued by Chris and Laura Mercogliano They returned the paper to its biweekly formatting in 2015, hiring Craig Low as publisher and Shoshanna McCollum as editor.

LAURA AND CHRIS MERCOGLIANO
Courtesy of the Mercoglianos

Today's *Fire Island News* carries on the tradition of featuring stories about problems and solutions unique to the island. The dilemma of beach erosion is an ongoing concern and will continue to be so—a barrier beach island being a barrier beach island. "New York's best kept secret," may not be so well-kept these days given the increase in the number of day-trippers and the problems they bring. Their rowdy behavior has even caused ferry cancellations. The periodic and most unfortunate fires that continue to threaten the island's already fragile environment are fought by the diligent and courageous fire departments as they were in yore. Book reviews, history and politics are covered as well.

The paper also reports on the joys of island living, (with glorious full color photos to prove it). Articles range from the goings-on of the LBGTQ community in Cherry Grove, to the mundane, but ever important, issue of recycling in Kismet (everywhere really, especially in these days of disposable water bottles of which we all seem so fond). Theatrical activities, parades, art fairs, lobster fests, barefoot kids, and the ubiquitous sand in beds, are all dutifully reported, creating memories with which residents will be regaling their grandkids.

The paper even has an ongoing history column reporting on the lost anecdotes of old.

Like most of us, the paper has bulked up some—60 pages or so—with advertizing up from 30% to 45%. Full page, full color ads for beers and real estate, ads for restaurants, places to stay, more beer ads, essential services (or not), theater presentations, retail establishments, all vie for attention. Thanks to Northwell Health the paper is now free.

The *Fire Island News* is the real deal, and its readers should be thankful for continued access to such a valuable and entertaining asset.

Thank you Chris and Laura Mercogliano.

www.ingramcontent.com/pod-product-compliance
Lightning Source LLC
Chambersburg PA
CBHW070021100426
42740CB00013B/2574